THE GRAMMAR OF JUSTIFICATION

AN INTERPRETATION OF
WITTGENSTEIN'S PHILOSOPHY OF LANGUAGE

THE GRAMMAR OF JUSTIFICATION

An Interpretation of
Wittgenstein's Philosophy of Language

JOHN T. E. RICHARDSON

SUSSEX UNIVERSITY PRESS
1976

Published for
Sussex University Press
by
Chatto & Windus Ltd
40 William IV Street
London WC2N 4DF

*

Clarke, Irwin & Co. Ltd
Toronto

ISBN 0 85621 051 x

© John T. E. Richardson 1976

Printed in Great Britain by
REDWOOD BURN LIMITED
Trowbridge & Esher

CONTENTS

ACKNOWLEDGEMENTS

The author and publishers wish to thank the following for permission to reproduce extracts from the works of Ludwig Wittgenstein: Basil Blackwell and Mott Ltd, and Barnes and Noble Inc. for *The Blue and Brown Books (Preliminary Studies for the "Philosophical Investigations"); Notebooks 1914-1916* Ed. G.H. von Wright and G.E.M. Anscombe. Trans. G.E.M. Anscombe; *Philosophische Bemerkungen.* Trans. R.M. White and R. Hargreaves; *Philosophical Grammar.* Ed. R. Rhees. Trans. A.J.P. Kenny; *Philosophical Investigations.* Ed. G.E.M. Anscombe and R. Rhees. Trans. G.E.M. Anscombe; *Remarks on the Foundations of Mathematics.* Ed. G.H. von Wright, R. Rhees and G.E.M. Anscombe. Trans. G.E.M. Anscombe; *Zettel.* Ed. G.E.M. Anscombe and G.H. von Wright. Trans. G.E.M. Anscombe; Routledge and Kegan Paul, Ltd and Humanities Press, Inc. for *Tractatus Logico-Philosophicus.* Trans. D.F. Pears and B.F. McGuinness.

We are also grateful to Frederick Ungar Publishing Co. Inc. for permission to quote from *Introduction to Mathematical Thinking* by F. Waismann, and Oxford University Press and P.M.S. Hacker for permission to quote from *Insight and Illusion: Wittgenstein on Philosophy and the Metaphysics of Experience* © 1972.

PREFACE

In this essay, I hope to have written something of interest whatever the reader's familiarity with philosophical texts. For the recent student of philosophy, Wittgenstein is of course an interesting thinker in his own right, and I have tried to give a faithful account of his ideas, using his more explicit and unequivocal pronouncements and certain historical facts concerning his encounters with other philosophers in order to interpret his less explicit and more controversial remarks. In addition, his work includes extensive criticisms of other philosophers, and an important and influential discussion of what the activity of "doing philosophy" should comprise. For the more advanced scholar, I hope that the interpretation of Wittgenstein's philosophy of language which is given can be seen to be at the same time distinct from, and more developed than, the standard account which is usually offered by philosophers sympathetic to Wittgenstein. My exegesis is intended to be largely consistent with certain recent accounts of Wittgenstein's later philosophy, which interpret it as the general application of a constructivist framework. There are important debts which I owe to these accounts, and these are acknowledged here, and also in the introductory chapter to my essay.

Undoubtedly my highest gratitude is owed to Drs. Peter Hacker and Gordon Baker, of St. John's College, Oxford, whose lectures, papers, and personal advice are responsible for my enduring interest in philosophy. Dr. Baker's own research is the source of my motivation to study Wittgenstein's philosophy of language, and it would be difficult to overestimate what I owe to his profound scholarship.

The perceptive comments made by him and by Dr. Hacker on this and earlier versions of my essay are greatly appreciated.

Much of the groundwork for this research was carried out at the Center for Human Information Processing in the University of California, San Diego, where I was supported during the academic year 1970-1971 by U.S. Public Health Service grant MH 15828 from the National Institute of Mental Health. I am very grateful to Professor George Mandler and his staff for their hospitality. While at UCSD, I was fortunate to have discussions in seminar with Professors Henry Alexander and Avrum Stroll, and with Al Martinich, David Cole, Wayne Stromberg, and Michael White. Professor Alexander's criticisms are particularly appreciated.

At The University of Sussex, where I studied from 1971 until 1973, I was grateful for the comments and criticisms made by Professor Roy Edgley, Dr. Aaron Sloman, and Miss Jane Singleton, on previous versions of this essay. I am also grateful to Mr. Andrew Brennan, of the University of Stirling.

I have translated quotations from *Ludwig Wittgenstein und der Wiener Kreis,* but for other works I have used the published translations. I am particularly grateful to Basil Blackwell and Mott, Ltd., for permission to use advance copies of the translations of *Philosophische Bemerkungen* and *Philosophische Grammatik* by R.M. White and R. Hargreaves, and by A.J.P. Kenny, respectively.

Finally, I should like to thank Ludwig Wittgenstein for being so profoundly obscure as to make the exegesis of his philosophy a deeply satisfying intellectual activity.

Neuropsychology Unit,   John T.E. Richardson
Department of Neurology,
The Churchill Hospital,
Oxford.
1974

LIST OF ABBREVIATIONS

The following abbreviations are used to refer to
Wittgenstein's writings:

NB	*Notebooks 1914-1916*
TLP	*Tractatus Logico-Philosophicus*
WWK	*Ludwig Wittgenstein und der Wiener Kreis*
PB	*Philosophische Bemerkungen*
Moore	"Wittgenstein's Lectures in 1930-33"
PG	*Philosophische Grammatik*
BB	*The Blue and Brown Books*
NL	"Notes for Lectures on 'Private Experience' and 'Sense Data'"
RFM	*Remarks on the Foundations of Mathematics*
PI	*Philosophical Investigations*
Z	*Zettel*
OC	*On Certainty*

Full details of all these references are to be found in the
Bibliography.

A single insight at the start is worth more than ever so many somewhere in the middle.

LUDWIG WITTGENSTEIN

Chapter I

INTRODUCTION

In attempting to understand the writings of a particular philosopher, certain historical facts concerning experiences during his life-time may be helpful, or even crucial, in arriving at a correct interpretation. They may enable one to determine those philosophers who influenced him, those whom he influenced in his turn, and those who were the targets for his criticisms. Of course, the mere fact that philosopher A met philosopher B on such-and-such a date does not constitute evidence that either had any philosophical influence upon the other at all, but in some cases there may be a clear indication that a particular occurrence was important in determining the subsequent direction of a person's writings. When Ludwig Wittgenstein had completed his *Tractatus Logico-Philosophicus* around the end of World War I, he retired from the active study of philosophy, but only to return approximately ten years later. Now, it has been known for many years that his return to philosophy was not the result of some gradual re-awakening of interest in the subject; in fact, he was apparently reluctant to take part in any of the philosophical discussions organized by the Vienna Circle.[1] On the contrary, Wittgenstein's return to active philosophizing was precipitated by one particular event. This was a lecture which was given by the Dutch mathematician and philosopher of mathematics, L.E.J. Brouwer, at the invitation of the Vienna Circle, in March, 1928.[2] The content of this lecture and its effect upon Wittgenstein will be considered presently. For the moment, however, one should consider two points. The first is that this single event was responsible for Wittgenstein's taking up philosophy again after ten years' absence.

The second is that the philosophy which he went on to develop turned out to be markedly different from the ideas which he had expounded in the early stages of his career. For, despite the arguments for some degree of continuity and unity in Wittgenstein's thought throughout his life, the early and later philosophies differ radically in their method, in their style, and in their tone. Now, when one considers these two points, there are many questions which one would like to ask. The most obvious one is why Brouwer's lecture should have had such a profound effect upon Wittgenstein. One would like to know, further, how the contents of the lecture bore upon his early work, especially upon the *Tractatus,* which he had apparently left as a conclusive, definitive solution, or, at least, as a programme for such a solution, to all philosophical problems. Before having heard Brouwer's paper, Wittgenstein had shown no inclination at all to re-consider his early work. (In a letter to Schlick in 1925, he even claimed that he himself had no copy of the *Tractatus.*[3]) On the other hand, one would also like to know what the relationship is between the things which Brouwer had to say in 1928, and the philosophy which Wittgenstein subsequently developed. There is a variety of possible roles which Brouwer's ideas might play in Wittgenstein's later philosophy. They might form the cornerstones of the latter's arguments, or they might have merely an ancillary role. It is possible that Wittgenstein exploited Brouwer's ideas for some time, but abandoned them when they had lost their usefulness. Or Brouwer's lecture might have served merely as some kind of catalyst: something to fire off Wittgenstein's imagination, but not something to be itself represented in any way in the product of his subsequent philosophizing.

These questions are of obvious importance. As I attempted to indicate above, this is not a matter simply of writing an interesting account of the history of certain ideas, but of being able to produce a coherent and faithful interpretation of Wittgenstein's philosophy. But, despite the importance of these questions, it is a remarkable fact that very few philosophers have even bothered to ask them, let alone to suggest sensible answers. This surprising omission cannot be accounted for on the ground of a lack of primary sources, for Brouwer's paper was published in the *Monatshefte für Mathematik und Physik* in the following year. Nor is it true to say that scholars interested in Wittgenstein's ideas have been unwilling to dig up his past; for recent years have seen a fair amount of philosophical archaeology in this direction.[4] However, I have no particular wish to pursue the psychological and sociological causes which have determined the current study of Wittgenstein's thought. For the present, I merely wish to point this out as a somewhat surprising neglect of possibly fruitful material. In this essay, I would like to attempt to show that many ideas to be found in Wittgenstein's later philosophical writings can be seen as deriving from the ideas expounded by Brouwer in his Vienna lecture. Some of these ideas, I believe, are fundamental in arriving at a correct interpretation of Wittgenstein's later philosophy. In particular, I would like to suggest that his later conception of what a philosopher ought to be doing is dictated almost entirely by a view of language and human activity which he took over from Brouwer. This conception of philosophy will be considered in Chapter II. I would then like to argue that Wittgenstein's later philosophy of language also has its source in these ideas, and to suggest a particular interpretation of his semantic theory on the basis of this argument. This refers to the idea that the meaning of a word or sentence is determined by its "use", and is to be found in Chapter III. Finally, I hope to show that certain topics of discussion in Wittgenstein's later writings can be seen to relate intimately to this philosophy of language, and to support the interpretation which I have given. The particular topics which I shall consider will be the discussion of family resemblance and of concepts with broad borderlines (Chapter IV), and the discussion of the concept of a criterion (Chapter V).

Before embarking upon this essay proper, I would like to give due credit to the previous research which has considered the influence of Brouwer's ideas in Wittgenstein's later philosophy, and which has inspired and directed my own work. The basic theme of this essay is that Wittgenstein's later philosophy consists of the elaboration of a theory of meaning which belongs to the family of semantic theories which has been called "constructivism". According to such theories, the meaning of a sentence is to be explained in terms of the conditions which are regarded as appropriate for its employment; for example, the meaning of a declarative sentence is to be explained in terms of the conditions which are recognized as evidence for its truth, where at least some of those conditions must be believed or known to hold by the utterer of such a sentence in order for him to be competent to assert it. Such a theory will be explained in more detail in Chapters II and III. It is opposed to the more standard "realist" theory of meaning, according to which the meaning of a sentence is to be explained in terms of the fact which would make some "corresponding" declarative sentence a true sentence. This distinction between realism and constructivism, and the general interpretation of Wittgenstein's writings which I shall give here, derive originally from the work of Michael Dummett. In his review of Wittgenstein's *Remarks on the Foundations of Mathematics,* Dummett was able to point out the thoroughgoing constructivist approach which is to be found in that work. Since then, he has produced a series of papers which share as a common theme the investigation of the implications of a generalization of constructivism to all domains of philosophical discussion.[5] Dummett calls this position "anti-realism", but it is a restricted form of constructivism insofar as it explains meaning in terms of the conditions for *conclusive* justification of employment.

SUSSEX UNIVERSITY PRESS

have pleasure in sending herewith for review

TITLE THE GRAMMAR OF JUSTIFICATION

AUTHOR John T. Richardson

PRICE £6.00

PUBLICATION DATE 8th April, 1976

Sussex University Press request that NO *review shall be allowed to appear before the day of publication.*

They would also very much appreciate a copy of any review that you may give.

40–42 William IV Street
London WC2N 4DF

Telephone: 01–836 0127

In his doctoral dissertation at the University of Oxford,[6] Gordon P. Baker attempted, amongst other things, to portray the kind of logical system which would underlie a generalization of constructivism, and to indicate the consequences of this position for philosophy in general. He interpreted Wittgenstein's later philosophy as a general critique of the fundamental semantic principles of the *Tractatus,* and as the development of a radically different alternative approach. Pursuing an implication of Dummett's work, Baker emphasized the important influence of Brouwer's ideas upon Wittgenstein, and also attempted to indicate the precise chronological pattern in which Wittgenstein's later philosophy developed. He adduced certain consequences of his account for the interpretation of Wittgenstein's philosophy of language, and it was in attempting to criticize and develop such remarks that I was led to the accounts of family resemblance and of the idea of a criterion which form the second half of this essay. The emphasis upon the justification of assertions which runs through these chapters is taken from Baker's work, though, in Chapter III, I voice some reservations as to whether this should be identified as a fundamental notion for the purposes of conceptual analysis.

A recent book by P. M. S. Hacker, *Insight and Illusion: Wittgenstein on Philosophy and the Metaphysics of Experience,* includes an account of the ideas contained in Brouwer's lecture, and a discussion of the reasons why Wittgenstein should have found them so profoundly exciting in terms of his previous ideas (pp. 98-104). Hacker mentions in particular the influence of Schopenhauer and Frege upon Wittgenstein's earlier writings, and he points out that Brouwer's approach constituted a direct attack upon the Fregean, realist semantics of the *Tractatus* from a firmly Schopenhauerian position. He cites as precursors both Dummett and Baker, and interprets from a constructivist standpoint Wittgenstein's attack upon solipsism and upon the possibility of a private language, and his discussions of avowals and of criteria.

Another recent work, *Perception, Sensation, and Verification,* by Bede Rundle, starts from the distinction between realism and anti-realism which was made by Michael Dummett, and investigates how these approaches fare in the case of the problem of other minds. Unfortunately, although Rundle starts his book by considering Wittgenstein's position as a "partial" anti-realism, according to which the justification for assertions need not be logically conclusive (p. 8), he subsequently appears to oppose the concept of evidence to that of direct, conclusive verification, and says that only the latter is relevant to meaning, that anything short of *proof* is uninteresting (pp. 16, 36, 74). He also suggests that, insofar as statements ascribing certain mental predicates may be verified solely on the basis of a person's behaviour, such predicates are not to be regarded as paradigmatically mental (p. 31). However, I hope to show that on Wittgenstein's account to suppose that verification must always be conclusive is to be the victim of a realist dogma; and that it is a consequence of his particular form of constructivism that the sense of *any* mental predicate is to be explained in terms of the behaviour characteristic of that predicate. So, although it is true that Rundle develops in considerable detail one possible form of constructivism, and elaborates the opposition between this and a particular realist position, he only considers this restricted (anti-realist) form, and, moreover, it seems that he judges the issue by means of realist criteria.

Finally, John L. Pollock considers a constructivist approach to the treatment of propositions concerning physical objects ("Criteria and our Knowledge of the Material World"). He starts by emphasizing the notion of the justification for knowledge-claims, and suggests that this will be more useful than conventional philosophical "analysis". The meaning of a concept is to be explained, on this view, by the set of conditions which justify the ascription of the concept to an object. Pollock suggests that propositions concerning physical objects are to be justified by descriptions of subjective experience, and he calls this kind of justification, "criteria". In the fifth chapter of this essay, I shall point out that such a notion is to be found in Wittgenstein's writings, but that he rejected this particular application of the term "criterion" on the grounds that evidence must be public. So, while Pollock's paper identifies a semantic relation which is fundamental to Wittgenstein's philosophy, the application which he makes of this relation is not one which accords well with the latter's ideas. (To be fair, to present such an application is by no means Pollock's purpose.) However, his paper does serve to point out the usefulness of a constructivist approach to philosophical problems, and to develop an important alternative to Wittgenstein's treatment of a particular realm of discourse.

The purpose of my own study is to complement the previous work in Wittgenstein's logic, his philosophy of mathematics, and his metaphysics of experience by, respectively, Baker, Dummett, and Hacker, in order to argue for a constructivist interpretation of his writings. My intentions here are exegetical, rather than critical; I wish simply to attempt to give a more or less perspicuous account of Wittgenstein's philosophy of language, in the belief that this will serve as a stepping-stone towards a successful global interpretation of his later philosophy.

Chapter II

WITTGENSTEIN ON PHILOSOPHY AND LANGUAGE

If one wishes to acquire a good understanding of a philosopher's writings, an essential prerequisite for this task is an appreciation of his conception of what philosophers ought to be doing. The literature already contains good accounts of Wittgenstein's later conception of philosophy, such as those by Fann[1] and by Hacker,[2] and I have no particular wish to disagree with the interpretations which they have given. However, in this chapter I would like to give a slightly different account, so as to suggest that this conception of philosophical activity sprang originally from one fundamental set of ideas.

These ideas are to be found in the lecture which Brouwer delivered in March, 1928.[3] (They are also to be found in a paper which he read to the tenth International Congress of Philosophy in 1940,[4] and in a paper on the intuitionistic conception of the philosophy of mathematics which Arend Heyting presented at a conference in Königsberg in 1930.[5]) In this paper, Brouwer made the suggestion that one should consider mathematics, science, and language as human activities with a social and historical context. They are, according to Brouwer, the principal functions by means of which mankind is able to govern nature and to maintain order in its midst; they are the manifestations of a basic will to live. In order to express this will, to impose it upon others, and to secure their co-operation, mankind evolves systems of communication. At primitive stages of development, the transmission of the will can be brought about by means of gestures and noises, although pre-linguistic modes

18

of apprehension make possible the construction of abstract mathematical systems. In the case of more developed social organizations, an articulated language is required, and this is constructed by interpreting the elements of a mathematical system as basic linguistic signs, and by interpreting the rules of the system as grammatical rules which regulate the formation of utterances containing the signs. However, it is important to understand that organized language is the product of the free activity of human beings. It is conventionally adopted as a social instrument for the communication of thoughts, it has no absolute foundation, and may be modified or rejected at any time.

Brouwer's lecture appears to have been the only formal philosophical event at which Wittgenstein took part during his relationship with the Vienna Circle.[6] One member of the group has related how reluctant Wittgenstein was to attend the lecture at all, and it was evidently only after extreme persuasion that he heard Brouwer speak. Yet it also appears that this lecture had an extraordinary effect on Wittgenstein: "He became extremely voluble and began sketching ideas that were the beginnings of his later writings."[7] Why Brouwer's ideas should have had particular importance for Wittgenstein has been discussed by P.M.S. Hacker, in his book, *Insight and Illusion* (pp. 98-104). In this chapter, I would like to show how Brouwer's conception of language and of mankind dictates a particular view of what philosophy should consist in, and a particular attitude towards the activity which has been traditionally known as "philosophy". In the following chapter, I shall explore a theory of meaning which might be associated with Brouwer's ideas, to the effect that words derive their meanings from human linguistic activity, from their use in everyday life. However, in both cases, these accounts will be presented as interpretations of Wittgenstein's own writings, under the assumption that his ideas do indeed have their origin in the Brouwer lecture. This assumption will

19

be supported by demonstrating connections between the tenets of Wittgenstein's philosophy and the ideas proposed by Brouwer, and by the cohesive picture of Wittgenstein's writings which, I hope, will result.

First of all, consider that, on Brouwer's conception, language is the interpretation of an abstract mathematical system. It follows that research into the foundations of mathematics will have important consequences in the philosophical study of other realms of discourse, as Brouwer himself observes.[8] A recurring theme of this chapter and the next will be that this idea was taken up by Wittgenstein, so that his philosophy of language is reflected in his philosophy of mathematics, and vice versa. Consequently, the interpretation and exegesis of one will assist in that of the other. Wittgenstein himself sometimes refers to mathematics as "the language" (e.g. *WWK*, pp. 104, 170). Second, if grammatical conventions play the role of rules in an abstract system, then the notion of following a rule will represent an important connection between the philosophy of language and the philosophy of mathematics. Wittgenstein gives an extended discussion of this concept in the *Philosophical Investigations* (§§ 143-240). Third, following a rule is supposed to consist in an act of free choice, though of course no conscious decision or resolution need have occurred when somebody follows a rule (*BB*, p. 143). Wittgenstein asserts that, while one may feel compelled by a rule, it is equally important that one can choose to follow it (*RFM*, V, §45). Linguistic conventions are arbitrary rules adopted to regulate our discourse, and they represent the limit of justification. They may be used to criticize and justify, but they themselves cannot be justified, for there is no such thing as a justification in this case. All one can say is: "That is how we do it" (*BB*, p. 24; *Moore* II, p. 299; *PI*, §217; *RFM*, II, §74). Similarly, in the case of mathematics, the acceptance of a proof involves a decision to employ the proved proposition as a paradigm or rule, but it does not amount to a discovery about some mathematical reality (*RFM*, II, §§26-30).

On Brouwer's account, the existence of a language depends upon its usefulness in communicating desires and intentions, and in securing co-operation with other individuals. It therefore depends upon some amount of agreement between the members of a community with regard to the conventions which constitute the language. Such agreement is part of the framework on which the operation of language is based (*PI*, §§240-241). There must be, for example, agreement in certain fundamental judgements, in the employment of the colour vocabulary, in the results of mathematical calculations, and in the results of such techniques as measurement (*PI*, §242; p. 226; *RFM*, II, §§74-76). The idea of a consensus is an essential part of that of a technique (*RFM*, II, §§66-67). This agreement in turn will depend upon the relative permanence of physical objects. For example, the procedure of weighing a piece of cheese in order to determine its price would "lose its point" if it frequently happened that such lumps grew or shrank for no obvious reason (*PI*, §142). However, while it is the case that empirical facts concerning the permanence of material objects enable a human society to make a certain choice of concepts and techniques, they do not justify that choice. Although the technique of calculating is a part of natural history, its rules do not play the role of propositions of natural history which would be justified by appeal to such general empirical facts (*RFM*, V, §14). And while the proposition "12 inches = 1 foot" is grounded in a technique, it does not express the physical and physiological conditions that make the technique possible (*RFM*, V, §1). Nevertheless, language is an essentially social activity, and this is emphasized in a remark in the *Philosophical Investigations* (§199; see also §§198-205; *RFM*, II, §§36, 67): "It is not possible that there should have been only one occasion on which someone obeyed a rule. It is not possible that there should have been only one occasion on which a report was made, an order given or understood; and so on. — To obey a rule, to make a report, to give an order, to play a game of chess, are *customs* (uses, institutions)."

If language is a human creation, in the sense that it consists in the interpretation of a formal system, adopted for the purpose of communication with other people, then the sense of an individual linguistic symbol will be determined by the interpretation assigned to it in the course of human linguistic activity. In short, words have those meanings which human beings give them, a point which Wittgenstein asserts explicitly in the *Blue Book* (p. 27). Elsewhere, he remarks, for example, that the criteria of identity of a psychological experience are fixed by a human community (*PI*, § 322). Necessity in language is therefore simply a matter of the rules which the community decides to lay down; as Wittgenstein puts it: "The *must* corresponds to a track which I lay down in language" (*RFM*, II, § 30). Wittgenstein's view of the nature of language thus commits him to a conventionalist position over the idea of necessary truth. He suggests, for example, that we consider the following: "The only correlate in language to an intrinsic necessity is an arbitrary rule. It is the only thing which one can milk out of this intrinsic necessity into a proposition" (*PI*, § 372). He says that any language is founded upon convention, and that talk about "essence" merely consists in noting conventions (*PI*, § 355; *RFM*, I, § 74). For example, the statement, "You can't count through the whole series of cardinal numbers," does not state some fact about human frailty, but about a convention which human beings have made. It is not like a statement of some physical impossibility, but is similar to the statement, "There is no goal in an endurance race" (*BB*, p. 54; cf. *PI*, § 374).

Now, if traditional philosophy is regarded as the study

of putative substantive *a priori* truths, then it follows from the conception of language which is being described here that the assertions of traditional philosophers are, strictly speaking, nonsense. In fact, since language is to be regarded as a free creation of human beings, anything which is relevant to understanding the working of language and which might therefore be relevant to philosophy, is to be found in the conventions governing the employment of the language. But these are already in plain view (*WWK*, p. 183), and so if one wishes to know something about the meaning of a word, one simply has to observe and describe what is prescribed by these conventions. As Wittgenstein puts it, one simply has to "look and see" (*PI*, §§66, 340). He continually makes the general assertion that language can contain nothing that is hidden which could be of any interest to philosophers (e.g. *PI*, §§126. 435). The data of philosophical discussions are to be "observations which no one has doubted, but which have escaped remark only because they are always before our eyes" (*PI*, §415; *RFM*, I, §141). The aspects of things that are most important for philosophical considerations are only "hidden" because of their simplicity and familiarity (*PI*, §129). The problems of philosophy are not of the kind which can be solved by discovering new information. On the contrary, it is "of the essence of our investigation that we do not seek to learn anything *new* by it. We want to *understand* something that is already in plain view" (*PI*, §§89, 109; see also *BB*, p. 6). Philosophy is to be concerned with those linguistic conventions which are jointly and freely adopted by the members of a particular society. It is therefore to be of such a nature that if anyone tried to advance philosophical theses, "it would never be possible to debate them, because everyone would agree to them" (*PI*, §128; see also *PG*, §89; *PI*, §599; *WWK*, p. 183). In particular, there is no hidden "essence" which can be brought to light by some process of analysis (*PG*, §35; *PI*, §§91-92, 97). As

23

was indicated above, "essence" is expressed in linguistic conventions, or, to use Wittgenstein's term, it is expressed by *grammar* (*PI*, § 371). In general, metaphysics is reduced to the study of language: everything metaphysical is to be found in grammar (*Z*, § 55); and a metaphysical proposition can always be re-expressed so as to show that it hides a grammatical rule (*BB*, p. 55).

On the one hand, philosophy is to consist in the clarification of ordinary language. On the other hand, the basic data of philosophy are to be empirical facts about language whose truth is to be self-evident. But is there not a deep contradiction here? If everything lies open before us in plain view, how do we get involved in philosophical problems? Wittgenstein explains that we are misled in part by the simplicity and familiarity of the very things that are important (*PI*, § 129). Further, because of the particular forms of expression which we find in our own language, we acquire strong prejudices concerning the way in which language functions (*BB*, p. 43; *Z*, § 323). We are not able to rid ourselves of "the implications of our symbolism" (*BB*, p. 108). Consequently, we approach language from the wrong side, and so we no longer know our way about (*PI*, § 203). Wittgenstein remarks that when we do philosophy we are like savages who put false interpretations upon the utterances of civilized men, and draw the strangest conclusions (*PI*, § 194). However, the most important reason why we are misled concerning the true nature of language is that its superficial aspect, its "clothing", makes different words appear similar in function, and so we remain unconscious of the prodigious diversity of our everyday language-games (*PI*, p. 224). Like the handles in the cabin of a locomotive, the words of a language look more or less alike, but in fact have very different kinds of application (*PG*, § 20, *PI*, § 12). The misunderstandings which we have to try to clear away are caused by our mistakenly assimilating different language-games, by our being misled by certain analogies between the forms of expression in different regions of language (*PI*, §90). Wittgenstein gives many examples of the kind of confusion which he has in mind. We are misled, for instance, by the similarities between thinking and bodily activities, and then we mistakenly search for a locus of mental activities (*BB*, pp. 7, 16). Again, we are misled by the analogy between measuring physical distance and measuring time, or that between a change in physical location and a change in temporal location, and we ask: How is it possible to measure something which is not present (*BB*, pp. 26, 107-108)? Another example is the similarity (and the lack of similarity) between having toothache and having a gold tooth: a person may have toothache, and they may have a gold tooth, but in the latter case the possession is alienable, in the former case, inalienable (*BB*, pp. 49, 53).[9] Another case is the confusion between properties and ingredients of objects; although it is true that to ascribe the property of being alcoholic to beer is to say that it includes alcohol as an ingredient, it is not the case that beauty is an ingredient of things which have the property of being beautiful (*BB*, pp. 17, 144). Finally, there is the confusion between propositions expressing physical impossibilities, and propositions expressing logical impossibilities (*BB*, p. 56). The confusion generated here is at the root of all philosophical problems, for the characteristic of a metaphysical question, according to Wittgenstein, is that it expresses an unclarity about the grammar of words in the form of a scientific question (*BB*, p. 35). In Zettel (§438), Wittgenstein explains this as follows: "The essential thing about metaphysics: it obliterates the distinction between factual and conceptual investigations."

When we are misled by the analogies between different uses of a word, it is important to determine how far these analogies go (*BB*, p. 23). It will often be found that the analogy is merely superficial, and that there are fundamental "grammatical" differences. Now, the idea that logical relationships between linguistic items will not be reflected faithfully in their superficial representation is by no means novel. It is to be found in Frege and Russell, and plays an important role in Wittgenstein's early work (e.g. *TLP*, 4.002, 4.0031). But in his later philosophy, these relationships are not themselves "hidden" in any sense; they are part of the "linguistic competence" of any speaker of the language. The problem lies not in finding these relationships, but in paying due attention to them, and not being distracted by surface analogies. In the *Remarks on the Foundations of Mathematics* (I, § 108), Wittgenstein uses the expression, "the superficial form of our grammar", to refer to this surface appearance, but in the *Investigations* (§ 664) it is explained more fully:

> In the use of words one might distinguish "surface grammar" from "depth grammar". What immediately impresses itself upon us about the use of a word is the way it is used in the construction of the sentence, the part of its use—one might say—that can be taken in by the ear.—And now compare the depth grammar, say of the word "to mean", with what its surface grammar would lead us to suspect. No wonder we find it difficult to know our way about.

The misunderstandings which are characteristic of traditional philosophy come about because of a failure to command a clear view of the use of words (*PI*, § 122). The kinds of prejudice which were mentioned above, concerning the way in which language is supposed to function, surround the actual working of language with a haze which makes clear vision impossible (*PI*, § 5). Above all, Wittgenstein says, our grammar is lacking in perspicuity (*PB*, § 1; *PI*, § 122). What we must do in order to put matters right, is to take what is already open to view, and to make it surveyable by a rearrangement (*PI*, § 92). We must strive for a synoptic, comparative account of the class of concepts which presents difficulty (*Z*, §§ 273, 464). However, the order which is to be sought in our knowledge of the use of language is not *the* order, but one out of many possible orders; it is an order with a particular end in view, that of clearing away misunderstandings (*PI*, § 132). By attaining a clear view of our language we can remove all of the assertions of traditional philosophy; we can pass from something that is disguised nonsense to something that is patent nonsense (*PI*, §§ 464, 524). So, in attempting to remove philosophical misunderstandings, the concept of a perspicuous representation is of fundamental importance (*PI*, § 122). An example of a perspicuous representation of grammatical relationships which Wittgenstein himself cites is the colour octahedron as a representation of the use of colour words (*PB*, § 1). However, philosophical misunderstandings come about in a wide variety of ways, and so the methods of philosophy must be just as various; as Wittgenstein remarks, "The complexity of philosophy is not in its matter, but in our tangled understanding" (*PB*, § 2; see also *Z*, § 452). The job of the philosopher is thus to remove our "intellectual discomfort" by a synopsis of many trivialities (*Moore* III, p. 27). His work is to consist in assembling reminders (*PI*, § 127), but this is to be done "for a particular purpose", that of dispelling illusion, and not for its own sake. For this activity of producing a perspicuous description of linguistic usage gets its purpose only from the philosophical problems which it is supposed to remove (*PI*, § 109). G.E. Moore reported that Wittgenstein used to criticize philosophers who dealt with linguistic points of no bearing upon philosophy (*Moore* I, pp. 5-6; III, p. 27). However, the precise relationship between linguistics and philosophy will be considered in more detail later in this chapter.

Wittgenstein illustrates his way of doing philosophy by the analogy of a jig-saw puzzle:

It seems to us as though we had either the wrong pieces, or not enough of them, to put together our jig-saw puzzle. But they are all there, only all mixed up; and there is a further analogy between the jig-saw puzzle and our case: It's no use trying to apply force in fitting pieces together. All we should do is to look at them *carefully* and arrange them (*BB*, p. 46).

The conception of philosophy in Wittgenstein's later writings is radically different from, and totally opposed to, the traditional activity which is known by that name. Indeed, he suggests that it might be misleading to call what he does "philosophy" at all. Rather, one might say that the subject with which he deals is "one of the heirs of the subject which used to be called 'philosophy' " (*BB*, p. 28). Philosophy, on Wittgenstein's account, is to consist in the removal of misunderstandings from discourse, the untying of knots in our thinking, the uncovering of nonsense. It is to be the battle against the bewitchment of our intelligence by means of language, the fight against the fascination which forms of expression exert upon us (*BB*, p. 27; *PI*, § 109). The questions which are asked by traditional philosophers are not real questions which might be answered by supplying some information; rather, they are expressions of unclarity, of mental discomfort (*BB*, p. 26). The problems which are posed are not scientific problems; indeed, Wittgenstein remarks that the very word "problem" is misapplied when used to refer to our philosophical troubles (*BB*, pp. 6, 46). They are to be seen as muddles which are felt to be problems, and which arise when language "goes on holiday" (*BB*, p.6; *PI*, § 38). According to Wittgenstein's conception of philosophy, the aim will be to make these "problems" disappear by clarifying ordinary linguistic usage (*PG*, § 72; *PI*, § 133; *RFM*, V, § 13). This will allow us to appreciate empirical facts about language without being misled by our distorting spectacles (*PI*, §103). In the *Blue Book* (p. 43), he summarizes an actual application of this approach as follows: "The scrutiny of the grammar of the word weakens the position of certain fixed standards of our expression which had prevented us from seeing facts with unbiassed eyes. Our investigation tried to remove this bias, which forces us to think that the facts *must* conform to certain pictures embedded in our language."

The central idea in Wittgenstein's later approach to his subject is that philosophy is to consist in the identification and removal of the source of intellectual puzzlement and discomfort (*BB*, p. 59). Now, it is readily seen that the practice of this kind of activity will bear various similarities to the diagnosis and treatment of an illness. Wittgenstein suggests that the main cause of philosophical disease is "a one-sided diet: one nourishes one's thinking with only one kind of example" (*PI*, §593). Elsewhere, he remarks: "What a mathematician is inclined to say about the objectivity and reality of mathematical facts, is not a philosophy of mathematics, but something for philosophical *treatment*. The philosopher's treatment of a question is like the treatment of an illness" (*PI*, §§254-255). And he talks of "curing" philosophers of "the temptation to attack common sense" (*BB*, p. 59). One can extend the analogy even further, by assimilating the philosophical method, as prescribed by Wittgenstein, to psychoanalysis. John Wisdom is, of course, the chief proponent of this idea.[10] Although Farrell's characterization of Wittgenstein's conception of philosophy as "therapeutic positivism" is said to have found little favour with him,[11] the similarities between the Wittgensteinean method and that of psychoanalysis are reasonably obvious, and several passages in his later writing make explicit comparisons.

The philosopher is the man who has to cure himself

of many sicknesses of the understanding before he can arrive at the notions of the sound human understanding.

If in the midst of life we are in death, so in sanity we are surrounded by madness (*RFM*, IV, § 53).

The sickness of a time is cured by an alteration in the mode of life of human beings, and it was possible for the sickness of philosophical problems to get cured only through a changed mode of thought and of life, not through a medicine invented by an individual (*RFM*, Appx. II, § 4).

In philosophizing we may not *terminate* a disease of thought. It must run its natural course, and *slow* cure is all important (*Z*, § 382).

There are, however, some important disanalogies between psychoanalysis and Wittgenstein's later conception of philosophy. In Norman Malcolm's *Memoir* (pp. 56-57), Wittgenstein is reported as saying that the two are "different techniques", but it is not clear what he had in mind. In the *Investigations*, Wittgenstein remarks that "there is not *one* philosophical method, though there are indeed methods, like different therapies" (*PI*, § 133). Any method may be used, even that which used to be called "analysis", that is, the substitution of one form of expression for another, so long as this assists in clarification and does not itself lead to more misunderstanding (*PI*, §§ 90-91). Further, the philosophical disease is not itself without value. For example, he says that philosophical problems have the character of depth: their significance is as great as the importance of our language (*PI*, § 111). In *Zettel* (§ 460), there is the following remark: "In a certain sense one cannot take too much care in handling philosophical mistakes, they contain so much truth." The prejudice which prevents us from simply looking at a word's use is not a stupid prejudice (*PI*, §340). The result of our philosophizing may be what we knew all the time, but the search is worth more than the discovery (*Z*, §457). The value in the discovery of nonsense is the deeper insight into language which it brings.

Possibly the most important difference between Wittgenstein's technique and psychoanalysis is that the latter is, or is supported by, a scientific theory which attempts to explain the aetiology of the psychiatric condition. This theory gives a preconceived conceptual framework in which to characterize the condition, and it makes general assertions and assumptions about the course of cognitive development. But in philosophy, Wittgenstein maintains, we are not to look for scientific theories. A word simply has the meaning which it is given by its user, and so there can be no scientific investigation into what it "really" means (*BB*, p. 28). That the method of philosophy is quite different from the method of science is something which he had maintained in his early philosophy (see, e.g., *NB*, p. 93; *TLP*, 4.111-4.1122), and, in the Philosophical Investigations (§109), he reaffirms this position:

> It was true to say that our considerations could not be scientific ones. It was not of any possible interest to find out empirically "that, contrary to our preconceived ideas, it is possible to think such-and-such" —whatever that might mean. (The conception of thought as a gaseous medium.) And we may not advance any kind of theory. There must not be anything hypothetical in our considerations. We must do away with all *explanation*, and description alone must take its place.

In the *Blue Book* (p. 18), he says that the tendency to assimilate philosophy to science is the real source of metaphysics, and leads the philosopher into complete darkness.

However, because the conception of language as a set of freely adopted conventions entails the proposition that any linguistic facts which are relevant to philosophy are already open to view, the idea that philosophy is to consist of descriptions, not of explanations, is taken to an extreme (e.g. *BB*, pp. 18, 125; *PI*, §§ 109, 124, 126, 496; *Z*, §§ 220, 314-315). In philosophy, Wittgenstein says, we are not to draw any conclusions, nor are we to make any assertions: we can only state what everyone admits (*PI*, § 599; *WWK*, p. 186). We are not attempting to make any discoveries, for the solutions to philosophical problems can never be surprising (*WWK*, pp. 182-183). Prejudices concerning the way in which language works have already been identified as a major source of philosophical confusion, and in general we must have no preconceived ideas to which linguistic facts must correspond (*PI*, § 131). Philosophical statements are to be arrived at as the result of investigation; they are not to take the form of requirements to be imposed upon that investigation (*PI*, § 107). Only a radical break with our preconceptions will lead to the disappearance of philosophical paradoxes (*PI*, § 304). Wittgenstein remarks: "We want to replace wild conjectures and explanations by a quiet weighing of linguistic facts" (*Z*, § 447). Unfortunately, because most people who study philosophy are imbued with the traditional conception of that activity, the great difficulty in carrying out investigations according to Wittgenstein's approach will be that of accepting as a solution to a problem a description of linguistic facts which looks as if it were only a preliminary to a solution (*Z*, § 314). But our remarks are not even to be hints of explanations, indirect means of reaching something which is hidden (*BB*, p. 125). They are simply, one might say, observations on the natural history of human beings, although it is true that we can also invent fictitious natural history for comparison (*PI*, § 415; p. 230). Now, this is the position that philosophy leaves everything as it is, and it has two important consequences (*PI,* § 124). The first is that it is no part of philosophical activity to give a foundation to language. Being freely created, it requires no justification. The second consequence is that no philosophical criticism of language is possible: "ordinary language is all right" (*BB,* p. 28; see also *PI,* § 98). Although it is true that ordinary language can be reformed for practical purposes, it is not for philosophy to interfere in this manner (*PI,* § 132); and no more scruples are justified over our language than a chess-player has over chess, namely, none (*PG,* § 77).

On Wittgenstein's view, therefore, the role of philosophy is to give a perspicuous description of the linguistic conventions employed by a particular community in order to remove the philosophical puzzlement of the members of that community. These conventions will determine the correctness or otherwise of the employment of particular linguistic expressions in particular circumstances. In the case of declarative sentences, they determine the conditions under which such sentences may be justifiably asserted, the grounds which are recognized as supporting such assertions. This kind of general semantic theory will be explored in the remainder of this essay. Now, it has been observed by Michael Dummett in several papers (e.g. "The Reality of the Past"; "Truth"; "Wittgenstein's Philosophy of Mathematics") that this "constructivist" account of the meaning of declarative sentences is opposed to the more traditional "realist" account, which asserts that the rules governing the employment of words in a declarative sentence will determine what has to be the case for one to be able to use that sentence to make a true statement. On this latter theory, there is in general some objective state of affairs in virtue of which any statement is true or false; though whether or not these conditions obtain is something independent of our knowledge. Three features of

33

such a semantic theory are to be noted immediately. First, the realist conception of meaning assimilates all cases of assertion to the stating of facts about objects, i.e. the kind of assertion which states that a particular state of affairs holds with regard to a particular set of objects. In the case of sentences which do not obviously fit this model, the theory has to give an explanation of what kinds of object, what kinds of state of affairs, etc., the sentence is about. Second, the meaning of an individual word is to be explained in terms of those conditions which are individually necessary and jointly sufficient for the truth of statements correctly applying the word. Third, since meaning is explained in terms of truth-conditions, and since only declarative sentences are true or false, the realist theory of meaning has to give an analysis of the meaning of a non-declarative sentence as derivative upon some "corresponding" declarative sentence.[12] All three features involve some degree of explanation, based upon a preconceived idea concerning the way in which words and sentences acquire meaning.

The constructivist account limits the philosopher to describing the conventions which determine the appropriateness of particular utterances: he must describe, not explain. In the case of assertions, he must describe the grounds which are conventionally taken to justify such assertion. But there are many other uses of language, and he is not to make the mistake of assimilating these different language-games. He is not to assimilate non-assertive uses to assertive ones, nor is he to assimilate all assertive uses to the stating of facts about objects.[13] Further, since these conventions lay down the conditions which the speakers of a language recognize as justifying the appropriateness of an utterance, it must be the case that these conditions may be recognized by the speakers of a language as obtaining when they do obtain, and so the justifiability of an utterance is tied to the utterer's knowledge.

Certain aspects of a constructivist theory of meaning have already appeared in this chapter, but Wittgenstein's constructivism can be seen particularly clearly in his philosophy of mathematics. A realist position over mathematics is usually referred to as "platonism", and this claims that the facts which make our mathematical statements true or false are facts about a non-empirical realm of mathematical objects which exists independently of our knowledge of those objects. The meaning of a mathematical statement is to be explained in terms of the corresponding mathematical fact. On the other hand, a constructivist philosophy of mathematics maintains that the condition which justifies calling a mathematical proposition a theorem is that of having a proof of the proposition. Mathematics is seen as an activity in which one proceeds according to certain rules in the derivation of mathematical expressions, but the truth of those expressions consists in their having been proved, not in their corresponding to some mathematical fact. In his review of the *Remarks on the Foundations of Mathematics*, Dummett elaborates this distinction between platonism and constructivism, and also argues that Wittgenstein's own position may be seen as an extreme version of constructivism. Here, however, it will be sufficient to show that Wittgenstein's philosophy of mathematics bears certain affinities to constructivist philosophies, and to show how it reflects his general conception of philosophy. In the next chapter, it will be considered in more detail, in order to examine the importance for Wittgenstein of the concepts of mathematical proof and of the application of mathematical propositions.

Wittgenstein's attitude to platonism is particularly evident from the following remark: "Someone makes an addition to mathematics, gives new definitions and discovers new theorems—and in a *certain* respect he can be said not to know what he is doing.—He has a vague imagination of having *discovered* something like a space (at

35

which point he thinks of a room), of having opened up a kingdom, and when asked about it he would talk a great deal of nonsense" (*RFM*, IV, §5). Whether or not one believes in "mathematical *objects* and their queer properties" is irrelevant to how one actually does mathematics (ibid.). He criticizes Dedekind's platonism: "The misleading thing about Dedekind's conception is the idea that the real numbers are there spread out in the number line. They may be known or not; that does not matter. . . . This is a frightfully confusing picture" (*RFM*, IV, §37). In the *Philosophical Investigations* (pp. 226-227), he characterizes mathematics as an activity, as a set of techniques which are conventionally adopted to deal with, and to talk about, the physical world. This conception is obviously very close to that suggested by Brouwer in his 1928 lecture. Elsewhere, he expresses the fundamental tenet of a constructivist philosophy of mathematics: "The mathematician is an inventor, not a discoverer" (*RFM*, I, §167; see also I, §32; IV, §11; Appx. II, §9). Finally, a remark in the *Investigations* states that the mathematician's own philosophical tendencies are irrelevant, and may even be the subject for treatment (*PI*, §254).

As I have described it here, constructivism is a range of philosophies which includes intuitionism and various brands of finitism. As one might expect from the original influence of Brouwer, there are many similarities between Wittgenstein's writings and intuitionism, most particularly in the emphasis upon elementary computations as a fundamental mathematical paradigm, the discussion of Brouwer's problem concerning whether a particular sequence of digits appears in the expansion of π, and the discussion of the role of the Law of the Excluded Middle in mathematical (and other) reasoning. Wittgenstein criticizes the psychologistic foundations of intuitionism (*RFM*, III, §44), but there is a more radical difference between his ideas and previous philosophies of mathematics. This derives from the philosophical conservativism discussed earlier, which extends to mathematics just like any other realm of discourse. Philosophy "also leaves mathematics as it is, and no mathematical discovery can advance it. A 'leading problem of mathematical logic' is for us a problem of mathematics like any other" (*PI*, § 124). On the one hand, mathematics stands in no need of a foundation or justification. What mathematical propositions do stand in need of, just like any other kind of proposition, is a clarification of their grammar (*RFM*, V, § 13). In his book, *Introduction to Mathematical Thinking*, Friedrich Waismann gives an exposition of some ideas contained in an unpublished manuscript of Wittgenstein, and remarks:

> The expression "to found arithmetic" gives us a false picture, because it gives us the idea that its structure is to be erected on certain basic truths. Instead, arithmetic is a calculus which starts only from certain conventions but floats as freely as the solar system and rests on nothing.
>
> The conclusion which can be drawn from these considerations is that we can only describe arithmetic, namely, find its rules, not give a basis for them. Such a basis could not satisfy us, for the very reason that it must end sometime and then refer to something which can no longer be founded. Only the convention is the ultimate. Anything that looks like a foundation is, strictly speaking, already adulterated and must not satisfy us (pp. 121-122).

On the other hand, whereas other philosophers of mathematics have attempted a critique of mathematical reasoning, the exclusion of those parts of mathematical practice which do not fit certain criteria, and the reconstruction of mathematics on the basis of the remainder, Wittgenstein wishes only to clarify and understand mathematics as it is actually practised: [14]

The philosopher must twist and turn about so as to pass by the mathematical problems, and not run up against one,—which would have to be solved before he could go further.

His labour in philosophy is as it were an idleness in mathematics.

It is not that a new building has to be erected, or that a new bridge has to be built, but that the geography, *as it now is*, has to be judged.

We certainly see bits of the concepts, but we don't see the declivities by which one passes into others.

That is why it is of no use in the philosophy of mathematics to recast proofs in new forms. Although there is a strong temptation here.

Even 500 years ago a philosophy of mathematics was possible, a philosophy of what mathematics was then (*RFM*, IV, § 52).

He criticizes finitism for attempting to escape from philosophical confusion by denying the existence of something. "Thus I must say, not: 'We must not express ourselves like this', or 'That is absurd', or 'That is uninteresting', but: 'Test the justification of this expression in this way' " (*RFM*, Appx. II, § 18, cf. IV, § 36). Nor must we seek to make discoveries: it is not the business of philosophy to resolve a contradiction by means of some mathematical or logico-mathematical discovery, but to describe the present situation so as to achieve a clear view of the state of mathematics that causes confusion (*PI*, § 125; *RFM*, II, § 81). These remarks indicate that Wittgenstein's position on the philosophy of mathematics reflects his conception of philosophy in general, and they set it apart from all previous positions on the philosophy of mathematics, even those to which it might be expected to bear the closest affinities.

How is the philosopher to set about his task? What are the data for his consideration? Wittgenstein had concluded the *Tractatus Logico-Philosophicus* by describing what he saw as the correct method for philosophizing:

> The correct method in philosophy would really be the following: to say nothing except what can be said, i.e. propositions of natural science—i.e. something that has nothing to do with philosophy—and then, whenever someone else wanted to say something metaphysical, to demonstrate to him that he had failed to give a meaning to certain signs in his sentences. Although it would not be satisfying to the other person—he would not have the feeling that we were teaching him philosophy—this method would be the only strictly correct one (*TLP*, 6.53).

In a discussion with Waismann in December, 1931, he referred to this, saying:

> I once wrote: The only correct method of philosophizing would consist in saying nothing and leaving it to the other person to make assertions. I hold to that now. What the other person cannot do is to lay out the rules step by step and in the correct order, so that each question may be detached from all the others. . . .

> We cannot do anything else except *tabulate rules*. If by inquiring I have found that the other person sometimes recognizes these rules for a word, and sometimes recognizes those rules, then I say to him: Then you must distinguish exactly *how* you are employing it; *and there is nothing further I want to say* . . . .

> Thus I only point out to the other person what he is really doing, and I restrain myself from making any assertions. . . (*WWK*, pp. 183-186).

So Wittgenstein's is essentially a dialectic method, according to which the linguistic facts which we use in our philosophical considerations are to be elicited from the people suffering from illusion. After the discussion with Waismann, Wittgenstein made little explicit reference to such a technique, but the great majority of his philosophical writings, from the *Blue Book* onwards, is written in precisely this dialectic style, with Wittgenstein playing alternately patient and therapist. This style also reflects the personal nature of Wittgenstein's philosophy. Many of the mistakes made by the patient he himself had made at one time or another, and he had the utmost respect for those misled in such a manner.

Because the data for philosophical consideration are to be elicited from the minds of the bewildered, there will be no dispute with regard to their correctness. However, if one wishes to say that this is "the only correct method of philosophizing", one is then committed to an activity which is necessarily piecemeal, where different problems require distinct courses of therapy, and where the therapy has to be repeated for each individual who suffers from philosophical illusion. On the other hand, if one wishes for an activity which is comprehensive, which offers reasonably decisive arguments against the assertions of traditional philosophers, and which can be recorded at least in the form of case-histories to which anyone may refer, one then encounters the problem of validating even one's descriptions of ordinary linguistic usage. In the conversation with Waismann quoted above, Wittgenstein clearly adopted the former course, and there is reason to think that he continued to hold to this position throughout his later philosophy. In *Zettel* (§447), for example, he contrasts the two approaches as follows:

> Disquiet in philosophy might be said to arise from looking at philosophy wrongly, seeing it wrong,

namely as if it were divided into (infinite) longitudinal strips instead of into (finite) cross strips. This
inversion in our conception produces the *greatest*
difficulty So we try as it were to grasp the un-
limited strips and complain that it cannot be done
piecemeal. To be sure it cannot, if by a piece one
means an infinite longitudinal strip. But it may well
be done, if one means a cross-strip.—But in that
case we never get to the end of our work!—Of course
not, for it has no end.

However, in the same work, Wittgenstein appears to be
attracted to the "inverted conception" of philosophy which
he criticizes in this passage. In the case of mathematics, for
example, he wishes "a complete survey of everything that
may produce unclarity" (Z, §273). A large part of *Zettel*,
starting at Section 464, consists of an outline of a general
account of psychological concepts. He introduces this discussion by saying that he is concerned with the "pedigree" of
such concepts: "The treatment of all these phenomena of
mental life is not of importance to me because I am keen on
completeness. Rather because each one casts light on the correct treatment of *all*" (Z, §§464-465). In the *Blue Book*
(p. 44; cf. *PI*, §133), he talks of the "final picture", the
"final result", when all philosophical problems are solved,
without indicating that this goal is in principle unattainable.

Contemporary ordinary-language philosophy has almost
unanimously adopted a piecemeal approach with regard to
the subject-matter of philosophical writing, concerning
itself more with short papers on restricted subjects than
with a systematic and global approach to a whole class of
concepts. However, it has also assumed that its discussions,
restricted though they may be, are also relatively definitive.
The linguistic or conceptual statements which a philosopher
makes are intended to be accurate descriptions of ordinary
usage. But, as Wittgenstein seems to have been aware, this

41

then brings in the problem of validation. What kind of empirical evidence is a philosopher to collect, and whence is it to be derived? Wittgenstein is about the only philosopher to have even raised this problem, and it appears that he attempted to avoid it by restricting philosophy to a personal dialectic encounter. However, it should be observed that, while these problems have received little attention from philosophers, very similar ones are now commonplace in the field of linguistics, and there, even if the suggested solutions are unsatisfactory in various respects, the problem has received a good deal of discussion.

The question of the validation of philosophical statements is of fundamental importance, since it bears directly upon the range of statements which philosophers are entitled to make. But it is the limitation upon philosophical activity which is the feature of Wittgenstein's philosophy that is most difficult for contemporary philosophers to accept. That philosophy should not offer scientific or pseudo-scientific "explanations" is much less controversial than the position that philosophers can make no definitive statements about ordinary language, and that they are to offer no systematic accounts of their subject-matter. Hacker has criticized Wittgenstein's "neglect of architectonic considerations", and suggests that nothing in the latter's arguments "precludes comprehensive surviews of segments of grammar" (op. cit., pp. 139-144). Indeed, he argues that Waismann's attempted systematization of Wittgenstein's work in *The Principles of Linguistic Philosophy* shows that a piecemeal approach to philosophical writing is not an inevitable corollary of Wittgenstein's philosophy. But, while Hacker refers to the conversation with Waismann quoted above (i.e. *WWK*, pp. 182-186), he claims that the denial that there are any theses of doctrines in philosophy amounts to no more than the claim that clarification of grammar must always be obvious. In fact, as I have tried to indicate above, both of these points follow directly from the position that the dialectic method is the only correct way of doing philosophy. And the whole theme of this conversation is the distinction between a "dogmatic" approach, which consists in making assertions, and an "undogmatic" one, which consists only in pointing out to the person who suffers from philosophical bewilderment what he is really doing. A different argument is that if the curing of the sickness of the understanding is the sole purpose of philosophizing, then attempting to give an account of linguistic conventions for its own sake is no part of philosophy, nor is what Hacker calls "seeking a comprehensive surview of a segment of grammar which goes far and beyond what is necessary for purely therapeutic purposes." In fact, in the next chapter it will be seen that Wittgenstein regards the conception of language as a system of explicit conventions as, strictly speaking, incorrect. To conclude this discussion, however, it may be said that while Wittgenstein appears to have been unwilling to accept a completely piecemeal, unsystematic approach to philosophy, he also appears to have been conscious of the problems of the alternative approach. It can surely be no great criticism of him individually if he failed to solve a problem which other philosophers have failed even to consider.

I hope in this chapter to have shown that the research in the later half of Wittgenstein's life could have involved an investigation of the philosophical consequences of Brouwer's ideas on mathematics, science, and language. These include: a conception of philosophy as a therapy for misunderstandings concerning ordinary language; a conservativism with regard to the conventions of ordinary language; a constructivist, and hence conventionalist, account of the meaning of statements in ordinary language; a constructivist philosophy of mathematics; the rejection of traditional philosophy as nonsense; and a general belief in the absurdity of systematic philosophy. Each of these tenets reflects a range of positions which is consistent with the conception of language and mathematics as creations of the free will. In later chapters, Wittgenstein's position will be elaborated further, as we explore his own individual and original development of this basic constructivist philosophy.

Chapter III

MEANING AND USE

The directions which a constructivist theory of meaning would take were outlined briefly in the previous chapter. The central theme is that the sense of a sentence is determined by the circumstances which are conventionally taken to justify its utterance. In Wittgenstein's later writings, this idea is expressed as a point concerning the meaning of a sentence and its "use". Now, although many philosophers have referred in a favourable manner to the idea that the meaning of a sentence is determined by its use, few have tried to explain what it means, or what they think it means, to say this. It is possible that they have been discouraged by the fact that Wittgenstein sometimes seems to have regarded it as a tautology: "What is supposed to show what words signify, if not the kind of use they have?" (*PI*, § 10). However, he also appears to have realized that, precisely because it is tautological, one still has the task of spelling out exactly which aspects of a sentence's use are relevant to philosophical discussions about meaning. For example, in the *Remarks on the Foundations of Mathematics*, (V, § 7), he poses the obvious question: "It all depends *what* settled the sense of a proposition, what we choose to say settles its sense. The use of the signs must settle it; but what do we count as the use?—" In this chapter, I hope to show that Wittgenstein did attempt to give an answer to this question, and that a whole theory of meaning can be unpacked from the idea that meaning is determined by use.

The identification of meaning with "use in the language" is applied to words, symbols, phrases, expressions, and sentences (see, e.g., *BB,* p. 65; *PG,* §§ 23, 31; *PI,* §§ 30, 43,

45

138; p. 190; *RFM*, IV, §5). He asks: "Doesn't the fact that sentences have the same sense consist in their having the same *use*?" (*PI*, §20). He says that we should let the use of words teach us their meaning (*PI*, pp. 212, 220), and that it is the use of sounds and signs which makes them into language, which gives them life (*BB*, p. 4; *PB*, §54; cf. *PI*, §432). I have already mentioned the fact that Wittgenstein continually emphasizes the diversity of use of words in ordinary language; they are like the handles in the cabin of a locomotive, or the tools in a tool-box (e.g. *BB*, p. 67; *PB*, §13; *PG*, §§20, 31; *PI*, §§10-12). We must "make a radical break with the idea that language always functions in one way, always serves the same purpose: to convey thoughts—which may be about houses, pains, good and evil, or anything else you please" (*PI*, §304), a realist conception of language which he himself had held in the *Tractatus* (cf. *TLP*, 4-4.001; *PI*, §23).

Unfortunately, Wittgenstein's use of the term "use" is often extremely woolly and unsystematic. It includes many different notions which he does not effectively distinguish. One of these is the aim or purpose of language. In the *Philosophische Grammatik*, he denies that this is the aspect of meaning in which he is interested, although, he remarks, one might call a word's purpose its meaning in the sense in which one speaks of "the meaning of an event for our life". In this sense it would be a topic for scientific, i.e. linguistic or psychological, investigation, not one for philosophical investigation (*PG*, §§32-33). However, in the *Investigations,* he seems to think that the study of the aim of language will be illuminating: it is the aim or functioning of a word over which the philosopher must attain a clear view (*PI*, §5).

Another idea is the role which a word plays in the life of a community. This appears in the *Brown Book* (pp. 94, 102-103), where Wittgenstein says that whether a word in a language of one community is correctly translated by a word in the language of another community will depend upon whether the two words play the same role in the lives of the respective communities. He means to include here the occasions on which the words are used, the expressions of emotion and other forms of behaviour which generally accompany their use, and the ideas which prompt their utterance or are evoked by their utterance. In *Zettel* (§§532-534), he reiterates the idea that a concept is characterized by the position which it has in the life of a community, this time in the case of the concepts of pain, sorrow, and affection. Finally, in the *Grammatik* (§29), Wittgenstein emphasizes the infinitely various ways in which language interacts with life. Although the precise implications of this idea are not explicitly stated, the idea that language is a social activity rather than some abstract logical entity is a central part of constructivism, and one of the principal themes of Brouwer's 1928 lecture. One interpretation of the idea that the meaning of a word is determined by its role in the life of a community is that a word's meaning is determined by its application. This is particularly evident in Wittgenstein's later philosophy, and will be considered in detail presently.

Again, Wittgenstein often describes language and concepts as instruments (*BB*, pp. 67-68, 79; *PI*, §§291, 421, 492, 569). However, he remarks that the sense in which the invention of a language means the invention of an instrument for a particular purpose is different from that in which it is analogous to the invention of a game (*PG*, §140; *PI*, §492), and it is the latter with which Wittgenstein is mainly concerned, as will become evident later. This distinction may perhaps be better expressed as follows: although instruments have purposes, they also have "modes of employment" (cf. *PI*, §421); thus, a hammer may be used to make a bookcase, or it may be used to knock nails into wood. Now, although the concepts employed by a particular community reflect its interests, its aims, and its desires (*PI*, §570; *Z*, §§373-391), Wittgenstein is not especially interested in what language is used to do, but, rather, in how it is used. Other notions which are tied up with that of "use" include the function or functioning of a word, and the circumstances in which it is used (*BB*, p. 108; *PB*, §12; *PI*, §§5, 11, 21, 33, 559; *Z*, §118).

Nevertheless, there are three notions which can be distinguished with some degree of clarity, and at least two of these can be shown to be particularly fundamental to Wittgenstein's later theory of meaning. When he indulges in hand-waving and requires a single word to express his general approach, he uses *"Gebrauch"* (e.g. *PB*, §14; *PG*, §23; *PI*, §§10, 30, 43, 138, 432, 532, 556, 561; p. 212; *RFM*, IV, §5). It is this term which is used in the well-known remark at *Investigations*, Section 43: "For a *large* class of cases—though not for all—in which we employ the word 'meaning' it can be defined thus: the meaning of a word is its use in the language." It also occurs in the *Philosophische Grammatik* (§23): "The explanation of the meaning explains the use of the word. The use of a word in the language is its meaning." Now, this term nowhere receives any clear exposition, but it is equally uncertain whether it is supposed to carry any great philosophical weight. It does immediately evoke a constructivist conception of language, for the realist view is that meaning and use are separable, and that it is the word's meaning which regulates its use, and which is therefore logically prior to the use. This particular confrontation of realism and constructivism will be elaborated later in this chapter.

However, it does appear that a word's *Gebrauch* involves at least two other notions. One of these is the *Anwendung*, or application of a word, which refers to the connection between signs and the world. In the *Philosophische Bemerkungen* (§54; see also §14), Wittgenstein says: "By application I understand what makes the combination of sounds or marks into a language at all. In the sense that it is the application which makes the rod with marks on it into a *measuring rod*: *putting* language *up against* reality." Just as an arrow only points insofar as a living being makes that application of it (*PI*, § 454), so words only have meaning in the course of their application and interpretation (*Z*, § 135). The meaning of a symbol lies in the technique of applying it (*PI*, § 557), and if a word has two distinct applications, it has two meanings (*PI*, § 140). If philosophers do not pay sufficient attention to the applications of sentences, they may be tempted to count some quite useless thing as a proposition (*PI*, § 520). A recurring theme, which has its origins in the conversations with Waismann and also in the *Grammatik* (*PG*, § 25; *WWK*, p. 167), is that being able to apply a sentence is a criterion of understanding it. So, on the one hand, the meaning of an expression is determined by the public, social practice, whereby a community employs the expression in order to talk about the world, and generally to communicate with one another; and, on the other hand, one's understanding of an expression amounts to one's having mastered this conventionally adopted technique (*PI*, §§ 197-202).[1] This reaffirms Brouwer's conception of language as having its basis in the activity of a social community.

Wittgenstein also makes a distinction between a word's *Gebrauch* and its function in a language-game (*PI*, § 556). The employment of a word in a game he refers to as its *Verwendung* (*PI*, § 182). This has to do with the word's "role" in language (ibid.), a point which is expressed in several different ways. He talks of the place of a word in language or in grammar, the post at which it is stationed, its role in a system of language, even its role in the calculus (*BB*, p. 78; *PG*, §§ 23, 27; *PI*, §§ 29, 257). This includes such information as the semantic category to which a word is assigned (*PI*, § 29). He says that the role of a word in language is what has to be understood if we wish to resolve philosophical paradoxes (*PI*, § 182). An important idea, which figures throughout Wittgenstein's later writings, is the assimilation of the employment of a word in language to the employment of a piece in chess (*Z*, §440). The point of this analogy, which will be discussed further later in this chapter, is that games are activities which are specified by conventionally adopted rules (*PI*, §§197, 205, 567; *RFM*, I, §130). Consequently, the employment of a word is to be seen as regulated by the linguistic conventions of a particular community. This is expressed by saying that the rules for the use of a word determine its sense (*PG*, §133); *PI*, p. 147; cf. *OC*, §65; *Z*, §321). A description of these rules, for Wittgenstein, constitutes the *grammar* of the word (*PG*, §23).

However, from a constructivist point of view, such linguistic rules or conventions cannot be identified independently of their applications. For to say that the use of a word is regulated in a particular society by certain conventions is to say that the members of that society behave in a particular manner with regard to the word. (Of course, which kinds of behaviour are relevant will need to be spelled out, and this will be considered in a moment.) So, one might say, the rules for the use of a linguistic expression are constituted by the applications of that expression. However, if such rules are not ontologically independent of the practice of employing the expression, they cannot explain or justify that practice.[2] This point was made in the previous chapter, with references to remarks taken from Wittgenstein's later philosophy: all one can say is, "That is how we do it." Now, the practice of employing an expression, the technique of its application, is not simply a matter of the expression's being uttered under some circumstances rather than others: this would be merely an empirical regularity, not a rule. Rather, the applications of an expression include the use of normative statements to assert that conventions exist which regulate its employment; the teaching of the expression by means of both correct and incorrect examples; and, in general, the whole range of behaviour which goes along with the utterance of an expression, and which justifies saying that the use of the expression is regulated. (Compare Wittgenstein's concept of the role which a word plays in the life of a community, discussed above.) For example, Wittgenstein considers the behaviour characteristic of someone's obeying a rule and of someone's having made an error (*PI*, §§54, 206; cf. §§207-208). Although he makes no effort to spell out more fully the linguistic practices which might be held to constitute the existence of a grammatical rule, some account has been given of what is involved in saying, more generally, that a norm exists in a given society, by H.L.A. Hart in his book, *The Concept of Law* (pp. 9-11, 50-54). Hart distinguishes rules from habits on three counts: first, the deviation of a person from a rule is open to criticism; second, such deviation is regarded as good reason for criticism; and, third, some of the population in the community must look upon the behaviour prescribed by the rule as a general standard to be followed by the community as a whole. In this context, Wittgenstein's constructivism appears when he remarks that, although a game is specified by its rules, the sense of sentences containing the name of the game is not determined unless the name is connected with the rules, and this connection is effected, "in the list of rules of the game, in the teaching, in the day-to-day practice of playing" (*PI*, §197; *RFM*, I, §130; see also *Z*, §302: "The rule . . . is what is explained, not what does the explaining").

As a provisional conclusion, it might be said that, on Wittgenstein's account, the *Verwendung* of a word is the set of rules governing its use (and this will include the internal relationships between the relevant concept and other concepts), but that it is in fact constituted by the word's *Anwendung*, the linguistic practices of the community in employing the word. Presently, further support for this account will be derived from a similar distinction between

Anwendung and *Verwendung* in Wittgenstein's philosophy of mathematics. However, it is interesting to note that these terms had similar, distinct, semi-technical usages in his early philosophy. In the *Tractatus*, Wittgenstein uses the term, *"Anwendung"*, to distinguish between primitive and derived signs. It refers to the mode of signification of a sign: whether it mirrors the world directly, or only *via* the signs which serve to define it (*TLP*, 3.26-3.262). On the other hand, he uses the term, *"Verwendung"*, to refer to the role of a sign in logical grammar (*TLP*, 3.325-3.328). He points out that confusion is produced by assimilating signs that have different roles, for example, names of objects and adjectives describing objects (*TLP*, 3.323-3.325; cf. *PI*, p. 176).

In the previous chapter, it was indicated that constructivism offers a particular account of the sense of declarative sentences: namely, the sense of a declarative sentence is constituted by the conditions which are conventionally taken to justify its assertion. In the first Appendix to the *Remarks on the Foundations of Mathematics* (§2), Wittgenstein discusses the concepts of truth and assertion. He points out that the great majority of sentences that we speak, write, and read, are declarative sentences (*Behauptungssätze*). We play the game of truth-functions with them. But, he remarks, the assertive use of such a sentence (i.e. the convention that in uttering such a sentence we generally attempt to make a true statement) is not something which is added to the sentence, but is an essential feature of the game which we play with it. This situation is comparable to that in chess, where there is winning and losing, and where it is the point of the game that each player attempts to win.[3] In the *Investigations* (§136), Wittgenstein puts this point by saying that the concept of truth "belongs" to the concept of a proposition but does not "fit" it. To give the correct account of the concept of truth, one has to ask something like: under what circumstances do we make an assertion? Or: how is assertion used in the language-game (*RFM*, Appx. I, § 6)?

Later in the *Remarks on the Foundations of Mathematics* (Appx. II, § 8), Wittgenstein remarks: "The proposition is worth as much as its grounds are. It supports as much as the grounds that support it do." This general connection between grounds and sense appears at many points in his later writings. In the *Blue Book* (p. 51), for example, he says that what characterizes the grammar of a proposition about physical objects is the kind of proposition which we regard as evidence for it. Elsewhere, he says that our having a concept is constituted by the fact that we take a particular sort of evidence to support a given judgment (*Z*, § 554). Asking whether and how a proposition can be verified yields a contribution to the grammar of the proposition; it tells us what sort of proposition it is (*PI*, § 353; *RFM*, V, § 29). What counts as an adequate test of a statement belongs to the description of the language-game (*OC*, § 82). An idea which is presented in the *Investigations* (§§ 472-486), and which is developed in *On Certainty* (e.g. §§ 83-93), is that certain propositions have a peculiar logical status because nothing is allowed to count as a negative ground, because everything speaks for them, and nothing against them. At *Zettel*, Section 437 (cf. *PI*, § 325), he distinguishes between the causes of belief and grounds: "The causes of our belief in a proposition are indeed irrelevant to the question what we believe. Not so the grounds, which are grammatically related to the proposition, and tell us what proposition it is." However, this evidential relation between the grounds and the proposition justified is not the same as strict entailment: the grounds for a belief are not propositions which logically imply what is believed (*PI*, § 481). In the passage from the *Blue Book* on the grammar of propositions about physical objects which was mentioned above, Wittgenstein remarks that, although

I may regard "I see my hand move" as one of the evidences for the proposition "my hand moves", "the truth of the latter is, of course, not presupposed in the truth of the former." My hand may appear to be moving without really moving, and we could even imagine cases in which the visual evidence is present and at the same time other evidences make us say that I have no hand (*BB*, pp. 51-52). So, although the evidential character of the grounds for an assertion is guaranteed by linguistic convention, they do not constitute conclusive evidence in the sense that they are not incontrovertible. This is the principal point of divergence between the constructivism to be found in Wittgenstein's later writings and the anti-realism which is expounded by Dummett, Rundle, and others.[4] The latter is essentially a constructivist framework, together with the requirement that all justification be conclusive. However, not only is the latter thesis a requirement, rather than a result, of investigation (cf. *PI*, § 109), but also it is in no way dictated by the adoption of a constructivist theory of meaning. Dummett gives no textual support for ascribing it to Wittgenstein, and Rundle even concedes that Wittgenstein's semantic theory is not anti-realist. Finally, justification must be essentially public and communal if it is to be determined by linguistic conventions; Wittgenstein makes this point as follows: "If I need a justification for using a word, it must also be one for someone else" (*PI*, § 378; cf. § 261).

Now, someone who adopts the position that the grounds of an assertion determine its sense must go on to give an account of the non-assertive uses of language. One strategy is to argue that the assertive use of language is primary, and that other uses, other types of sentence, are to be elucidated in terms of the "corresponding" assertion or declarative sentence. This would involve similar arguments to those given by realist philosophers in order to support their assimilation of all uses of language to fact-stating. One might suggest an analogy with Wittgenstein's philosophy of mathematics, for in the *Blue Book* (p. 20), he makes the following remark:[5]

> If I wished to find out what sort of thing arithmetic is, I should be very content indeed to have investigated the case of a finite cardinal arithmetic. For
>
> (*a*) this would lead me on to all the more complicated cases,
>
> (*b*) a finite cardinal arithmetic is not incomplete, it has no gaps which are then filled in by the rest of arithmetic.

Similarly, it might be suggested, investigating assertion is quite satisfactory, since it will lead on to all the more complicated uses of language, but, on the other hand, the language-game with assertion is not incomplete. Subsequent research will be evaluated according to whether it offers a good account of assertion, and whether other uses of language have proved to be conveniently analyzable as derivative upon assertion. This is the kind of position taken by Gordon P. Baker in *The Logic of Vagueness*, and the kind of interpretation which he gives of Wittgenstein's semantics. Baker cites as the fundamental thesis of constructivism the proposition that sense is to be explained in terms of assertion, and he develops a propositional calculus based upon a basic evidential relation, E, holding between context-independent type-sentences. His chief evidence for ascribing to Wittgenstein the view that assertion is primary is the kind of remark described previously (e.g. *RFM*, Appx. I, §§2, 6), but nothing that Wittgenstein says entails that this is the only way in which sentences acquire sense, though it does strongly suggest that the sense of *declarative* sentences is to be explained in terms of their assertibility conditions. Further, the appropriate generalization of constructivism is not that given by Baker, but the position that the sense of a sentence is to be explained in terms of the circumstances of appropriate employment. This position includes Baker's constructivism as a special case, but it is clearly more general.

More important, Baker's interpretation does not do justice to some of Wittgenstein's most well-known pronouncements. As has been noted previously, he makes a point of emphasizing the variety of ways in which language is used. He says that there are "countless" kinds of sentence, and he reviews "the multiplicity of language-games" (*PI*, § 23). Further, he criticizes other philosophers for trying to impose an account upon language, not a result of investigation, but a requirement (*PI*, § 107). Making a statement and giving a command are different language-games (*PI*, § 21), and there appears to be no reason to think that the meaning assigned to a word in one game is at all relevant to the meaning assigned to it in another. Primitive languages are quite possible which consist only of orders, and such languages will not therefore be incomplete (*PI*, § 15). Finally, if the same type-sentence may occur in different language-games, e.g. a declarative sentence used to inform and as a line in a play, then the appropriate object of semantic analysis is not the type-sentence, but the sentence-in-use. On the other hand, some account must be given of why the different uses of a word or sentence are uses of the *same* word or sentence, and not simply uses of different but homophonic linguistic units. Although Wittgenstein does not offer much help here, one might suggest that different uses occur in the same game. Thus, one might have a language-game consisting of orders and reports (cf. *PI*, §§ 19, 21), and so imperative and declarative sentences involving the same words would occur in the same game, and would be related by the rules of the game.

However, an objection may be put forward to either of these accounts. Surely, it may be asked, is it not the case that Wittgenstein continually attacks the notion that we use language according to strict rules, and, instead, emphasizes the role of explanation by examples? A direct reply is to point out that an example must be an example of *something*, and so it must be possible to give a criterion by which a given object can be accepted or rejected as such an example. The same rule need not be applied for all putative examples, but if there is no rule, there can be no justification, and, *a fortiori*, no exclusion. And an example of *anything* is not an example at all. So, on this account, when Wittgenstein objects to the notion of a strict rule, the emphasis is to be put on "strict" and not on "rule". But is it even true to say that he criticizes the philosophical strategy of regarding language as an activity proceeding according to strict rules? The most obvious passage to which one might refer is in the *Blue Book* (p. 25). Wittgenstein reminds us that language is neither used nor taught according to strict rules, and then remarks: "*We*, in our discussions on the other hand, constantly compare language with a calculus proceeding according to exact rules. This is a very one-sided way of looking at language. In practice we very rarely use language as such a calculus. . . . Our ordinary use of language conforms to this standard of exactness only in rare cases." But, if this is supposed to be a *criticism* of a way of doing philosophy, why does he use the pronoun "we"? He asks, why do *we* in philosophizing constantly compare our use of words with one following exact rules? "The answer is that the puzzles which we try to remove always spring from just this attitude towards language" (*BB*, p. 26). So, whether or not "we" are right in doing so, we conceive of language as an activity proceeding according to strict rules because that is the conception of those experiencing philosophical bewilderment, an idea which is worked out and illustrated by examples in the pages of the *Blue Book* which follow this passage.

The situation is clarified somewhat by considering some

remarks in the *Philosophische Grammatik*, which was written just before Wittgenstein began to dictate the *Blue Book*. In fact, several passages from this work are very similar to the remarks which have just been quoted. For example, Wittgenstein says that he is interested in meaning in a particular sense: in this sense, meaning is what is established when the meaning of a word is explained (§§ 23, 32). This is that sense of "meaning", he claims, which will allow us to clear up disagreement and misunderstandings (§ 24). Soon afterwards, he remarks: "But we look at games and language under the guise of a game played according to rules. That is, we are always *comparing* language with a procedure of that kind" (§ 26). In Section 32, he emphasizes the variety of kinds of game. There are games with well-developed systems of rules, such as football and cricket; there are primitive games, such as that where each person tries to throw a ball as high as he can; and, finally, there is the case where children simply throw a ball to each other. "Perhaps one will be unwilling to call some of these ball games at all," Wittgenstein says, "but is it clear where the boundary is to be drawn here?" However, he then says: "We are interested in language as a procedure according to explicit rules, because philosophical problems are misunderstandings which must be removed by clarification of the rules according to which we are inclined to use words. We consider language from one point of view only." Wittgenstein then proceeds to criticize alternative conceptions of meaning; but at no point does he suggest that having such a "one-sided point of view" ("*einseitiger Standpunkt*") is at all unsatisfactory. Presently, in Section 35, he remarks that we might draw limits to the use of a word for the purpose of resolving a philosophical paradox, and in Section 36 he explains this further:

If we look at the actual use of a word, what we see is something constantly fluctuating. In our investigations we set over against this fluctuation something more fixed, just as one paints a stationary picture of the constantly altering fact of the landscape.

When we study language we envisage it as a game with fixed rules. We compare it with, and measure it against, a game of that kind.

If for our purposes we wish to regulate the use of a word by definite rules, then alongside its fluctuating use we set a different use by codifying one of its characteristic aspects.

Similar remarks are to be found elsewhere in Wittgenstein's writings. Thus, he says that we can give concepts sharp boundaries for the purposes of explication and of the avoidance of misunderstandings (*PG*, § 76). We do this by making up several exact usages which together approximate to the actual use (*BB*, pp. 27-28). In *Zettel* (§ 467), he remarks: "Our investigation does not try to *find* the real, exact meaning of words; though we do often *give* words exact meanings in the course of our investigation." So, Wittgenstein suggests that the appropriate strategy is to conceive of language as an activity proceeding according to precise rules, and then to clarify the rules which one's philosophical opponents, those who are proposing theories, are using in their discourse. But this concept of language is not to be justified by showing it to be a "correct" account of language; indeed, Wittgenstein regards it as patently mistaken. It is justified solely by its success in removing misunderstandings and disagreements, in showing philosophical problems to be pseudo-problems, in removing the source of illusion. The recommended concept of language is correct pragmatically, not absolutely. In reality the conventions of ordinary language may be uncertain and fluctuating, as we shall see in the following two chapters.

How one-sided this conception of language is, can be

seen by examining those conceptions which Wittgenstein regards as inconsistent with it. G.E. Moore reports that in giving an account of meaning, Wittgenstein added that the sense in which he intended to use the word, "meaning", was only one of those in which we commonly use it (*Moore* I, p. 6). In *Zettel* (§ 143), he emphasizes the variety of things that might be relevant to the study of meaning:

> We might say: in all cases what one means by "thought" is what is *alive* in the sentence. That without which it is dead, a mere sequence of sounds or written shapes.
>
> If however I were to speak in the same way of a something that gives meaning to a configuration of chess pieces, that is to say distinguishes them from any old arrangement of little bits of wood—couldn't I mean all sorts of things? The rules that make the chess arrangement into a situation in a game; the special experiences that we associate with such positions in a game; the usefulness of the game.

Throughout his later writings, Wittgenstein criticizes several alternative conceptions of meaning, but he also points out that they might be useful for different purposes. For instance, when he says that the meaning of a word is what is established in an explanation of its meaning, this is intended to characterize a conception of meaning which is opposed to the conception of meaning as a characteristic feeling which accompanies the use of a word. This would be a scientific explanation, in that a causal relationship would exist between the explanation of meaning and the supposed characteristic feeling (*PG*, § 23; see also *BB*, p. 65; *Moore* I, p. 6). It might be relevant to an account of exclamations such as "hurrah", which evince, but do not refer to, feelings. Yet, Wittgenstein suggests, it would be inadequate to handle more central uses of language (*PG*, § 31). Similarly, meaning-as-use is to be opposed to meaning-as-purpose. An account of ejaculations might be given in terms of their purpose, e.g. saying "Boo!" might be used to surprise somebody. But the purpose of a word in ordinary language is again only causally related to its meaning (*PG*, § 32). Indeed, one might always invent new effects which the use of a sign might have (*PG*, § 33). In general, Wittgenstein is not interested in a psychological explanation of language. Such an explanation "stands outside the calculus; but we need an explanation which is part of the calculus" (*PG*, § 33). A rather different theory of meaning is that according to which the relationship between a word and its meaning is the same as that between a name and its bearer. Wittgenstein criticizes this theory in several places (e.g. *PI*, §§ 37-45, 55-59). It is ascribed to Augustine in the opening sections of the *Investigations* and elsewhere (*PI*, §§ 1-4; see also *PG*, §§ 19-20), and Wittgenstein identifies it as the underlying semantic theory of the *Tractatus* (*PG*, § 20). He says that it is clearly incorrect as a general theory of meaning, but that its importance lies in the fact that it gives a correct account of a narrowly circumscribed region of language. A limited definition can be extremely important to us (*BB*, pp. 18-19).

All these different conceptions can be useful for different purposes. But—to resume the earlier discussion—for the purpose of doing philosophy, i.e. for the purpose of carrying out the activity characterized in the previous chapter, the appropriate conception is that which sees language as a rule-governed activity, and which sees the meaning of a word as determined by the rules for its use. Thus language is to be assimilated to a game played according to explicit rules (*PG*, § 32). By "explicit", Wittgenstein appears to mean "definite", or "can be rendered explicitly". For, elsewhere, he points out that the expression of a rule need not actually be employed in a game, that one could learn a game without ever learning or formulating rules. But the rules may be "read off" from the practice of the game, using the behaviour which is characteristic of mistakes and of correct play (*PI*, §§31, 54). Understanding a game is demonstrated by correct play, not by being able to recite the rules (*PG*, §26; cf. *PI*, §78). Similarly, one learns the use of words under certain circumstances, but one does not learn to describe these circumstances (*Z*, §114). Consequently, it is possible that the speakers of a language would give a quite inadequate description of the concepts they employ (*Z*, §525). But, although they may not be able to enumerate the conditions under which a word is used, if a particular use is doubtful, they can say so, and why (*Z*, §118). So the "intuitions of the native speakers" will be relevant to philosophy, even if they cannot accurately articulate the use of words in their language.

I would now like to develop the discussion of Wittgenstein's views on the nature of mathematics. This can perhaps be best approached through the analogy between mathematics and a game, an analogy which is usually associated with the formalist school in the philosophy of mathematics. One of his earliest discussions of the analogy is contained in a critique of formalism which he dictated to Waismann in June, 1930 (*WWK*, pp. 103-105), and it is there attributed to Weyl. However, the idea itself goes back much further. Wittgenstein makes several references in his later work to Frege's extended criticism of formalism in the *Grundgesetze der Arithmetik* (Vol. II, §§86-137):[6] apart from the conversations with Waismann (*WWK*, pp. 105, 119, 130-136, 138, 150-152), it is mentioned both in the *Philosophische Grammatik* (§2; cf. p. 293), and in the *Blue Book* (p. 4). At the beginning of his criticism, Frege quotes the mathematician Thomae as follows:

The formal conception of numbers accepts more modest limitations than does the logical conception. It does not ask what numbers are and what they do, but rather what is demanded of them in arithmetic. For the formalist, arithmetic is a game with signs, which are called empty. That means they have no other content (in the calculating game) than they are assigned by their behaviour with respect to certain rules of combination (rules of the game). The chess player makes similar use of his pieces; he assigns them certain properties determining their behaviour in the game, and the pieces are only the external signs of this behaviour. To be sure, there is an important difference between arithmetic and chess. The rules of chess are arbitrary, the system of rules for arithmetic is such that by means of simple axioms the numbers can be referred to perceptual manifolds and can thus make important contribution to our knowledge of nature (§ 88).

Thomae's position is therefore that arithmetic is concerned only with the rules governing the manipulation of arithmetic signs. These rules are arbitrary in the sense that they are not justified by anything in the nature of numbers, but they are non-arbitrary in the sense that the signs manipulated according to them can be applied to the physical world. Frege disagrees (§§ 89-97), arguing that the rules of arithmetic are non-arbitrary, in that numerical signs refer to something objective, and that the nature of this objective reality justifies the rules of arithmetic. His argument runs as follows. It is the applicability of arithmetic which makes it a science, not just a game. But the equations of arithmetic can only be applied insofar as they express thoughts. The possibility of expressing a thought itself rests upon numerical signs having reference: configurations of signs in a formal system could no more express a thought than a configuration of chess-pieces. The use of referring signs in sentences expressing thoughts is regulated by their reference. That is, the reference of numerical signs supplies the grounds for the rules of arithmetic. Consequently, the rules of arithmetic are not arbitrary, but follow from the nature of numbers.

When considering the formalist position in the conversations with Waismann, Wittgenstein says that formalism contains an element of truth and an element of falsehood (*WWK*, pp. 103-105; see also p. 150). The element of truth is that any syntactic system can be interpreted as a system of rules for a game. The syntax of a language can only be distinguished from a game by its application; divorced from its applications, syntax is only a game, just like chess. The element of falsehood, contained in some brands of formalism, is the idea that mathematics therefore has to do with signs, with marks on paper. The numbers of arithmetic are not signs. The sign "0" does not have the property of yielding the sign "1" when it is added to the sign "1". But, Wittgenstein remarks, Frege was wrong to think that there were only two possible positions: mathematics concerns marks on paper, or else these marks designate objects. There is a third possibility, which is sanctioned by some versions of formalism, that mathematical symbols are not signs, but neither do they designate objects. That there exists a third alternative, Wittgenstein suggests, is shown by the example of chess. This does not concern pieces of wood being moved about on a wooden board, but neither do the pieces of wood designate anything. The third alternative is to say that the pieces are employed according to the rules of the game; similarly the meaning of an arithmetic sign is determined by the rules which fix its employment.

Thus, Wittgenstein adopts a position similar to Thomae's in opposition to that of Frege. Now, the controversy over the analogy between mathematics and a game reflects a deeper division between platonist and constructivist philosophies of mathematics. For the controversy turns upon the question whether the rules of mathematics can be justified. Frege asserts that they are to be justified by reference to some objective reality. Thomae asserts that they cannot be justified, except insofar as they can be employed in talk about the real world. Wittgenstein adopts the latter position; he says: "Syntax cannot be given a foundation. It is therefore arbitrary" (*WWK,* p. 105). Frege asserts that the rules of arithmetic follow from the meaning of the signs, Wittgenstein asserts that the meaning of the signs is determined by the rules of the calculus. So, even by 1930, Wittgenstein had adopted a constructivist philosophy of mathematics. However, his subsequent work places somewhat less emphasis on the analogy between mathematics and a game, despite the continuing constructivist approach. For example, in the *Philosophische Grammatik* (pp. 289-295), he gives an extended discussion of the analogy, but he confines himself to pointing out similarities and dissimilarities, and the whole passage is somewhat inconclusive. Later writings exhibit even less interest. His *Remarks on the Foundations of Mathematics* does not contain any well-developed ideas along these lines, not even a recapitulation of his earlier thoughts on the matter. However, it does indicate a new analogy; what is analogous to chess is not the whole of mathematics, but each of the individual calculi which make up "the motley of mathematics". Thus, comparing the system of rational numbers with the system of cardinal numbers is like comparing two games, say, draughts and chess. Wittgenstein asks: "How do we compare games? By describing them—by describing one as a variation of another—by describing them and emphasizing their differences and analogies" (*RFM,* Appx. II, §§ 13-14). Also, he refers to Russell's system as a game, a language-game (*RFM,* Appx. I, § 7). A similar development occurs in his philosophy of language, and this will be considered presently.

Generally speaking, Wittgenstein's philosophy of mathematics mirrors his views on the meaning of sentences in ordinary language. For example, he says that the use (*Gebrauch*) of the signs in a mathematical proposition determines its sense (*RFM*, V, § 7). In an early discussion in the *Philosophische Bemerkungen* (§§ 152, 154), he claims that the system of rules defining a calculus at the same time determines the meanings of the signs contained in the calculus. Consequently, in the philosophical study of such a calculus, one could not discover any new rules, for this would change the calculus and hence change the meanings of the signs. In the same passage, he remarks: "What a mathematical proposition says is always what its proof proves. That is to say, it never says more than its proof proves." Later, in the *Remarks on the Foundations of Mathematics* (II, § 28), Wittgenstein says that a mathematical proof "constructs" a proposition. The connection between proof and sense comes out particularly in the first Appendix to this work, which concerns Gödel's proof, and the concepts of truth and provability. Two sections (§§ 2, 6) emphasizing the role of assertion in declarative sentences have already been mentioned in this chapter. In a later passage (§ 15), he remarks: "Whether something is rightly called the proposition '*X* is unprovable' depends on how we prove this proposition. The proof alone shews what counts as the criterion of unprovability. The proof is part of the system of operations, of the game, in which the proposition is used, and shews us its 'sense'." Elsewhere, Wittgenstein remarks that determining a proposition as an axiom, i.e. as justifiable neither by proof nor by experiment, fixes its employment (*Verwendung*), and hence its sense (*RFM*, III, § 3).

On the other hand, he also emphasizes the importance of the application of mathematical concepts and propositions. He remarks that a mathematical proof is an instrument, it is part of an institution, just like the standard metre in Paris (*RFM*, II, § 36). The mistake which Russell made in his philosophy of mathematics was that of not paying adequate attention to the applications of his formulae, of looking at language without looking at the language-game within which it is used (*RFM*, II, §29); V, §8). Wittgenstein says: "You do not understand the proposition so long as you have not found the application. . . . One can know a proof thoroughly and follow it step by step, and yet at the same time not *understand* what it was that was being proved." And one must not be deceived by "the verbal form" of the proposition into thinking that it has an application where none exists (*RFM*, IV, §25). Like Thomae and Frege, Wittgenstein asserts that the application of mathematics sets it apart from a mere game with signs (*RFM*, IV, §2). This is not to say that parts of mathematics may not have quite fanciful applications, only that there must be connections between the fanciful and the non-fanciful applications (*RFM*, IV, §5; V, §25). However, Wittgenstein also discusses whether applying or proving should be taken as a criterion of understanding, and whether the application of a proposition depends on what is accepted as a proof of the proposition (*RFM*, II, §61; IV, §45).

The distinction between these two lines of thought, between sense-as-proof and sense-as-application, comes out particularly in the following problem. We often say that a given mathematical proposition (e.g. Pythagoras' Theorem) has two or more proofs. If one wishes to retain an emphasis upon proof as a determiner of sense, it has to be shown how this position is consistent with having two proofs for the same proposition. During the *Bemerkungen* period, Wittgenstein held that the sense of a mathematical proposition is given entirely by its proof, and hence two different proofs prove two different propositions (*WWK*, p. 109). Conversely, proofs which prove the same thing may be translated into one another, and so they may be said to be the same proof (*PB*, §153). However, he later came to question this dogmatic attitude. In the *Remarks on the*

Foundations of Mathematics (II, §62), he says that in order to know that two proofs prove the same proposition, it is not enough that they meet in the same propositional sign. That they prove the same thing "must proceed from other connections." Elsewhere in that work he gives a more detailed statement of his position:

> That these proofs prove the same proposition means, e.g.: both demonstrate it as a suitable instrument for the same purpose.
>
> And the purpose is an allusion to something extra-mathematical.
>
> I once said: "If you want to know what a mathematical proposition says, look at what its proof proves." Now is there not both truth and falsehood in this? For is the sense, the point, of a mathematical proposition really clear as soon as we can follow the proof?
>
> When two proofs prove the same proposition it is possible to imagine circumstances in which the whole surrounding connecting these proofs fell away, so that they stood naked and alone, and there were no cause to say that they had a common point, proved the same proposition.
>
> One has only to imagine the proofs without the organism of application which envelopes and connects the two of them: as it were stark naked (*RFM*, V, §7).

So, although Wittgenstein originally held the position that the sense of a mathematical proposition is given entirely by its proof, he revises this to include the application of the proposition. Although his position is not completely clear from the above quotation, it would appear to be something like the following: two different proofs prove different propositions of pure mathematics, but these propositions may receive the same application, and so represent the same proposition of applied mathematics.

An important aspect of Wittgenstein's philosophy of

mathematics is that he regards mathematical propositions as *grammatical* propositions, as rules: they show what it makes sense to say (*RFM*, II, §§ 26, 28, 39). Mathematics, on this view, does not consist in a network of facts, but in a network of norms (*RFM*, V, § 46). For example, the principle of induction is simply a convention establishing the sense of the expression, "proved for all natural numbers".[7] Rather than containing any knowledge of reality, a proved mathematical proposition is the expression of the acceptance of a new measure of reality (*RFM*, II, § 26). Consequently, the things that are called mathematical propositions have only a "very superficial" relationship with what we normally call a "proposition" (*RFM*, Appx. I, § 4). Such an idea is already present in the discussion of the analogy of a game in the *Philosophische Grammatik* (p. 291). Wittgenstein remarks there that to say that mathematics is a game would point out the difference between mathematical propositions and empirical propositions. One might even say that an equation does not express a proposition at all, but is employed as a bridge between one (empirical) proposition and another. Thus the distinction between mathematics and a game would relate to the concept of an empirical proposition, and the role played by the expressions of mathematics in relation to such propositions. Later, Wittgenstein explains his position in more detail (*RFM*, V, § 3). Mathematics has to do with the internal relationships between empirical propositions. For example, "25 x 25 = 625" records a convention which is constituted or created by acts of inference, e.g. from "here are 25 x 25 nuts" to "here are 625 nuts". The equivalence between the two latter empirical propositions is set up in the grammar, i.e. in the system of linguistic conventions. By setting up the convention, "25 x 25 = 625", the sense of the proposition, "here are 625 nuts", is changed: whereas it was previously verifiable only by direct counting, it is now verifiable also by verifying the proposition that there are 25 x 25 nuts.[8] On this view of the nature of mathematical propositions, it is important that such propositions involve signs that already have some meaning before the convention is established: "I want to say: it is essential to mathematics that its signs are also employed in *mufti*. It is the use outside mathematics, and so the *meaning* of the signs that makes the sign-game into mathematics" (*RFM*, IV, § 2; cf. II, § 34).

However, if the mathematical proposition has the status of a convention, what role does its proof play? For, surely, conventions are arbitrary, they cannot be given any justification. Wittgenstein's answer appears to be that the proof of the proposition determines what is decided when the convention is adopted. It is the proof which convinces us. It shows the place where the proposition stands, it places the decision in a system of decisions. It is the proof which changes the grammar of our language, changes our concepts. The sense of mathematical propositions is to be read off from their proofs (*RFM*, II, §§ 25-39). Unfortunately, these remarks do not appear to solve the problem: either a convention is established by its instantiation in particular transitions between empirical propositions, or it is founded on its proof, but Wittgenstein does not show how it might rest upon both. The difficulty might arise in a breakdown of the analogy between mathematics and language. For example, in the *Investigations* (p. 220), there is the following remark: "Let the use of the words teach you their meaning. (Similarly one can often say in mathematics: let the *proof* teach you *what* was being proved.)" A similar remark occurs in Waismann's *Introduction to Mathematical Thinking*: "It is only the proof itself which tells us the meaning of the proposition. To generalize: if we wish to know what a proposition means, we can always ask, 'How do I know it?' Its meaning is determined by the answer to this question" (pp. 96-97).[9] These quotations strongly support the contention of the previous chapter that

Wittgenstein adopted a *general* constructivist approach, to be applied to mathematics and ordinary language alike. Further, it is directly in accord with the distinction between employment and application suggested earlier that the "use" which is analogous to mathematical proof in the remark from the *Investigations* is the *Verwendung*. (It is also to be noted that, just as the employment of a word fixes its place in the system of language, so the proof of a proposition fixes its place in a system of decisions.) The analogy employed here appears to be the following:

justification : empirical proposition : : proof : mathematical proposition.

However, if Wittgenstein wishes to carry through a conventionalist account of mathematical propositions, the appropriate analogy might be characterized as follows: the transition from "*x* is an unmarried man" to "x is a bachelor" instantiates a linguistic convention; similarly the transition from "here are 2 + 2 apples" to "here are 4 apples" instantiates a mathematical theorem. This is the idea which Wittgenstein appears to adopt, but in this case all the arguments for the arbitrary character of language and mathematics can be invoked to give the (totally unacceptable) conclusion that proof plays no role whatsoever in mathematics. Whereas originally Wittgenstein adopted the position that the sense of a mathematical proposition is determined by its proof, at the expense of ignoring the role of the application of mathematics, he appears in his later works to be committed to stressing the importance of application without being able to give any coherent account of mathematical proof at all. It is possible that the concepts of proof and application may be moved closer together in the context of the strict finitistic paradigms which Wittgenstein considers, but there is otherwise no obvious way of attempting to resolve the problem.

What becomes of the analogy between mathematics and

a game? Earlier, it was noted that Wittgenstein comes to restrict it to an individual mathematical system or calculus, and a similar change occurs in his philosophy of language. In the *Philosophische Grammatik*, he refers to a particular sub-system of language as a calculus or language-game (*PG*, §§19, 26, 31), and it is this latter term which has particular importance in his philosophy of language. There is some amount of disagreement among Wittgensteinean commentators over the precise force to be attached to the analogy, but fortunately Wittgenstein himself explains what he means by the term "language-game" at various points in his later writings (e.g. *BB*, pp. 17, 81; *PI*, §7), besides giving many examples (e.g. *PI*, §§1-10, 19-21, 48-54, etc.).

He distinguishes three uses of the term, though clearly feels them to be closely related to one another:

> I shall in the future again and again draw your attention to what I shall call language games. These are ways of using signs simpler than those in which we use the signs of our highly complicated everyday language. Language games are the forms of language with which a child begins to make use of words. The study of language games is the study of primitive forms of language or primitive languages (*BB*, p. 17).

The first sense distinguished here is that of *simplified versions of examples of usage in everyday language.* This sense is most intimately connected with Wittgenstein's conception of philosophy. We remove "the confusing background of highly complicated processes of thought" in order to get a better view of our concepts. It is clear that the activity of describing such simplified forms of language will be a means towards removing philosophical problems (*BB*, p. 17).

The second sense is that of *linguistic games with which a child learns his native language* (see also *BB*, p. 81; *PI*, §7). This sense is connected with the first in that he suggests that in order to become clear about our concepts it is useful to ask, how did we learn the meaning of this word (*PI*, §77). It is also obvious that simplified versions of ordinary language will be employed by children when they learn language. However, although Wittgenstein sometimes talks about how a word is learned rather than how it is used (e.g. *PB*, §6; *PI*, §77; *RFM*, I, §1; *Z*, §§114-117, 267), it is not clear that language-learning plays any critical role in his later philosophy. Because as a matter of fact we do learn language by being taught, teaching is one way of effecting a connection between the use of a word and the sense of sentences containing it (cf. *PI*, §197; *Z*, §419). Further, there is a connection between the concept of teaching and that of meaning (*Z*, §412). However, Wittgenstein was not interested in learning theory or child psychology (*BB*, p. 6; *Z*, §§66, 412), and it seems that he did not wish to rule out the possibility of innate knowledge.[10] For instance, in *The Logic of Vagueness*, Baker cites a passage from Wittgenstein's unpublished *Manuscript Volume* II (p. 68), where he declares: "The meaning of a sentence lies in the nomenclature. The nomenclature is independent of the *hypothesis* that we learned this name in this use—in our youth, perhaps. The historical (which is always hypothetical) cannot be of any importance here." So although the phenomenon of teaching may be interesting as the subject of philosophical discussion, it is not of any general significance.

The third sense of "language-game" is that of *primitive forms of language*. In this case we illuminate the actual use of words by inventing new uses. These "clear and simple" language-games are set up as objects of comparison which clarify our ordinary language not only by their similarities to actual usage but also by their dissimilarities (*BB*, p. 28; *PI*, §130). "A perspicuous representation produces just that understanding which consists in 'seeing connexions'. Hence the importance of finding and inventing *intermediate cases*" (*PI*, §122).

In all three cases, language-games are systems of human communication. Further, as was mentioned previously, one reason for using the term "game" was to stress that they are to be seen as systems of rules or conventions. But the point of using the term "language-game" goes beyond this. It is "meant to bring into prominence the fact that the *speaking* of language is part of an activity, or of a form of life" (*PI*, §23). We are not to confine our attention to the sentences used, but we are to examine the whole verbal and non-verbal context in which they are employed. (*BB*, pp. 208-109). Indeed, in *Zettel* (§§541-545), Wittgenstein maintains that a language-game is an extension of primitive, pre-linguistic behaviour. Clearly, an important reason for using the term is again to emphasize the social nature of language.

A language-game is complete. This is not to say that it is a complete account of actual language, but that it is a complete account of some linguistic system. Thus it might be said of Augustine's description of language that as the description of a natural phenomenon it is incomplete; but it may also be said that he completely describes a simpler game (*BB*, p. 77; cf. *PG*, §19). Nor is it to say that it may not be embellished: but the embellished game will be a different game (cf. *PB*, §154: "The edifice of rules must be *complete*"). Finally, to say that language-games are complete is not to say that one game may not be related to a fragment of another (*Z*, §648). Indeed, it is presumed that the complicated forms which actually occur in natural languages may be built up from these simpler forms; there is no discontinuity between simpler language-games and the more complicated variety (*BB*, p. 17). Language-games are intended to be complete as self-contained systems which it is possible to work out in complete detail (*BB*, pp. 79-80). To regard a language-game as a complete system of human communication it is often useful to imagine it to be the entire system of communication of a primitive tribe (*BB*, p. 81).

Language-games are activities involving the employment of signs, and from them are constituted the rules which determine the meaning of the signs. This is reflected in one of the earliest recorded uses of this analogy, in the Moore lectures, where Wittgenstein suggests that when we say, "This makes no sense", we mean, "This makes no sense *in this particular game" (Moore* II, p. 295). A similar remark is given in *Zettel* (§134), which also expresses Wittgenstein's conventionalism: "Do not say 'one cannot', but say instead: 'it doesn't exist in this game'." In the *Blue Book* (p. 50), he refers to "grammatical games". Elsewhere, he says that a concept is in its element within the language-game, it is constituted by a language-game (*OC*, §65; *Z*, §391). A sound only becomes a linguistic expression as it occurs in a particular language-game (*PI*, §261). The connection between language-games and the concept of evidence is given in the following remark: "A *ground* can only be produced *within* a game" (*PG*, §55). Further, the justification of a statement belongs to the description of the language-game (*OC*, §82). Thus, a language-game is an activity determined by a system of linguistic rules which specify those circumstances which are conventionally recognized as legitimate for the employment of a concept or set of concepts.

This completes my examination of the theory of meaning to be found in Wittgenstein's later writings. What I have described, it is true, is nothing like an adequate account of the meaning of linguistic utterances. This obviously has to be filled out by future research. But my intentions have been more limited. First, I wished to examine Wittgenstein's concept of "use", in order to give something more than a superficial account of what is meant by saying that meaning is use. This implicated the notions of the rules of use (which Wittgenstein calls "grammatical rules"), and of the application of a linguistic expression by a society. I suggested that these were related, in that the rules were conventions constituted by the cases of application.

My second task was to show how the concept of justification has an important place in Wittgenstein's later philosophy. What is involved in the concept of justification, which sense of "justification" is relevant, also needs to be spelled out. This will be postponed until Chapter V, which considers the concept of a criterion. The existence of a close relationship between criteria and justification will be fairly easy to demonstrate, and an examination of this semi-technical concept will throw at least some light on "the grammar of justification". Certain properties of the relationship between grounds and assertion have already been mentioned, however. These include the points that this relationship is established by linguistic convention, but that it is a relationship weaker than entailment, in that it is possible that the justifying proposition be true and yet the proposition justified be false.

Third, Wittgenstein's philosophy of mathematics offers an account of the meaning of mathematical propositions which at least bears certain analogies to his account of the meaning of empirical propositions. For example, the notion of justification operative in mathematics is that of proof. At the minimum, the consideration of his philosophy of mathematics supports the account given of the concept of "use", in that two or three notions can be distinguished and yet related under the heading of "use". The account of Wittgenstein's philosophy of mathematics which was given was somewhat one-sided in order to stress the ideas connected with the provability and applicability of mathematical propositions; but somewhat different accounts are readily available, such as Kielkopf's *Strict Finitism,* or Dummett's review, "Wittgenstein's Philosophy of Mathematics". However, the emphasis upon proof was considered to be incompatible with other constructivist strands in Wittgenstein's thought which emphasize the importance of the application of mathematics.

Finally, the concept of a language-game is of obvious importance in Wittgenstein's later philosophy. My account of the notion suggests that it does not capture any important ideas which are not to be found elsewhere in his writings, but that it serves to bring together a variety of positions or concepts. There is the emphasis upon rules, and the general analogy between language and a game. Insofar as the rules determine the game, the rules of grammar determine the sense of our utterances. There is also the stress upon the social, communal, public nature of language: it is the playing of the games, the application of our concepts, that gives them life.

The present chapter has brought to light an important characteristic of Wittgenstein's later conception of philosophy. This is the general pragmatic approach which runs through all his discussions. The stress upon justification, the conceptualization of language as a rule-governed activity, the description and identification of language-games are but approximations to the truth. They are approximations which are justified to the extent that they are useful towards the goal of philosophy, as characterized in the previous chapter. This comes out most clearly in the concept of a language-game, which may be an approximation to some actual linguistic practice, or which may be a pure invention with more or less distant relationships to actual usage. The reason why we study such primitive systems is in order to become clear about that usage, to dispel illusion, to disperse the fog surrounding the working of our language. That, for Wittgenstein, is the only criterion for the validity of a philosophical technique.

Chapter IV

FAMILY RESEMBLANCES AND BROAD BORDERLINES

Up to this point, this essay has concentrated upon the development of a theory of meaning, and upon showing that such a theory is to be found in Wittgenstein's later philosophy. I shall now consider various ways in which he attempts to apply these ideas. This chapter will consider his treatment of a problem in definition; more precisely, it will study his criticisms of the traditional idea that concepts are to be defined by giving the necessary and sufficient conditions of their correct application. The following chapter will consider his concept of a "criterion", and his discussion of the grammar of psychological concepts. However, my strategy in both cases will be of a boot-strapping nature. On the one hand, I shall use the discussions of the previous chapters in order to give an exegesis of these further passages. On the other hand, the interpretation of those passages will serve to support and consolidate the account of Wittgenstein's philosophy of language which I have already given.

As almost everyone who studies Wittgenstein knows, his attack on the traditional conception of definition takes the form of a discussion of "family resemblance". Although this term is usually associated with the well-known passage in the *Philosophical Investigations* (§§66-67), it is to be found elsewhere in Wittgenstein's writings. Possibly the earliest account is that given in the *Philosophische Grammatik* (§35), and this passage is, if anything, more developed than the *Investigations* version. It also approaches the problem from a somewhat different direction, and so I will take this discussion as my starting point. In the first part of the *Grammatik*, Wittgenstein discusses various problems with the concept of meaning. Some of these problems were mentioned in the previous chapter, where I considered some of the conceptions of meaning which Wittgenstein rejects as possible alternatives to his own. One conception which recurs several times in the early sections is the idea that understanding, knowing, and meaning consist in certain mental occurrences, states, or processes which accompany a person's use of a word. As I mentioned earlier, Wittgenstein's initial response to this kind of suggestion is to say that this is not the concept of understanding, etc., which he has in mind and which will enable us to remove philosophical bewilderment. In Section 35, however, he mentions this idea again, in order to investigate the presuppositions of this account of meaning.

First, he points out, any psychologistic theory of this nature must be able to handle the fact that there seems to be no one mental occurrence which accompanies every instance of the understanding of a word (for example, an image of an exemplar of the relevant concept). On the other hand, there appear to be several interrelated occurrences which may occur, but it is not the case that such occurrences have to be present in all cases of understanding, nor even in the majority of such cases. The conclusion which is usually drawn, Wittgenstein observes, is that what is essential to understanding is some unconscious mental occurrence which one can only investigate and comprehend with considerable difficulty. But, if one concludes that, because there is no conscious occurrence common to all cases of understanding, there must therefore be some unconscious mental occurrence common to all such cases, one is presupposing the general semantic principle that what justifies the application of a generic term is some characteristic common to all its exemplars. What the application of such a term involves is certainly a relationship between the exemplars, but, Wittgenstein suggests, this relationship need not be that of having some property in common. The exemplars may be related as in a chain, so that each is related to another by connecting links; and two neighbouring members can have features in common, while more remote ones need have nothing in common at all. So two exemplars may not resemble each other, yet they still may belong to the same conceptual family. And even in those cases where there is a feature common to all the members of the family, it need not be that which defines the concept. He then remarks: "Thus there is probably no single characteristic which is common to all the things we call games. But it can't be said either that 'game' just has several independent meanings (rather like the word 'bank'). What we call 'games' are procedures interrelated in various ways with many different transitions between one and another." Here one should notice that, although the account in the *Grammatik* is originally intended to apply to a range of human capacities and dispositions (he actually mentions "understanding", "thinking", "knowing", "believing", "wishing", "intending", and "expecting"), it is also supposed to apply to a quite different concept, that of a game.

In the *Blue Book* (p. 17), Wittgenstein suggests that in order to tackle philosophical problems it will be very useful to consider language-games. But, he says, our "craving for generality" makes it difficult for us to take this line of investigation. This craving for generality is the result of a number of tendencies associated with particular philosophical confusions. One of these is the tendency to look for something in common to all the entities which we commonly subsume under a general term. He explains: "We are inclined to think that there must be something in common to all games, say, and that this common property is the justification for applying the general term 'game' to the various games; whereas games form a *family* the members of which have family likenesses." He says that this idea of a general concept being a common property of its particular instances is a "primitive, too simple" idea of the structure of language. A couple of pages later (p. 19), he remarks that "the idea that in order to get clear about the meaning of a general term one had to find the common element in all its applications has shackled philosophical investigation." He proceeds from this to a discussion of human dispositions (pp. 20 ff.). He takes as an example the concept of expectation, and argues as follows: "If one asks what the different processes of expecting someone to tea have in common, the answer is that there is no single feature in common to all of them, though there are many common features overlapping. These cases of expectation form a family: they have family likenesses which are not clearly defined." As in the *Grammatik*, then, Wittgenstein uses a point about the concept of a game to illustrate a feature of a quite different kind of concept.

In the *Philosophical Investigations*, remarks of this nature are made in the course of a long discussion of the nature of language. In this case, they are employed to answer the criticism that talking about language-games does not tell us what is common to all the things that we call "language". What is important, Wittgenstein suggests, is that these phenomena are *related* to one another in many different ways, not that there is one thing in common which makes us use the same word for all. Returning to the analogy of a game, he says:

Don't say: "There *must* be something common, or they would not be called 'games' "—but *look and see* whether there is anything common to all.—For if you look at them you will not see something that is common to *all*, but similarities, relationships, and a whole series of them at that . . . .

I can think of no better expression to characterize these similarities than "family resemblances"; for the various resemblances between members of a family: build, features, colour of eyes, gait, temperament, etc. etc. overlap and criss-cross in the same way.—And I shall say: 'games' form a family (*PI*, §§ 66-67).

Before discussing these ideas further, it should be pointed out that although family resemblance has been given some amount of critical attention, Wittgenstein used a variety of other metaphors throughout his later philosophy. The passage from the *Grammatik* discussed above compared the members of a conceptual family to the links in a chain (*PG*, § 35). In the *Brown Book* and elsewhere, he likened the similarities between them to the fibres of a thread or rope; he says: "The rope consists of fibres, but it does not get its strength from any fibre which runs through it from one end to the other, but from the fact that there is a vast number of fibres overlapping" (*BB*, p. 87; see also *PI*, § 67; *Z*, § 26). The properties of particular examples are like the leaves of an artichoke, and we misguidedly believe that in order to find the real artichoke we must divest it of its leaves (*BB*, p. 125; *PI*, § 164). Finally, in the lectures recorded by G.E.Moore, Wittgenstein criticized Freud for supposing that there is something common to all jokes, and for supposing that this supposed common character is the meaning of "joke" (*Moore* III, pp. 20-21; cf. p. 17); "joke", like "proposition", "has a rainbow of meanings."

Two initial observations can be made upon the passages discussed above. First, the point of the discussion of family resemblance is to criticize and reject the idea that a concept need be defined in terms of necessary and sufficient conditions of application. That definition should take the form of such conditions has always been a common assumption in philosophy and related fields. In the *Investigations*, the particular target is Wittgenstein's own earlier work (*PI*, §65); for instance, the *Tractatus* maintained that the essence of a proposition is given by the general propositional form, which is what is common to all propositions (*TLP*, 5.47-5.471), and a similar point is made concerning the concept of number (*TLP*, 6.022). Both of these are singled out for treatment in the later work (*PI*, §§65-68, 135). Second, the criticism contained in the discussions of family resemblance itself rests upon the general philosophical principle that what governs the use of a term must be obvious. We must "look and see" whether there is anything common to all the activities which are called "games".

In the light of the conclusions of the previous chapter, it might be suggested that the similarities which constitute the family resemblance are the circumstances which are cited to justify the ascription of the concept. This is directly supported by a remark in the *Philosophische Grammatik*, where Wittgenstein expresses his point of view as follows: "It might be said that the use of the concept word or common noun is justified in this case because there are transitional cases between the members" (*PG*, §35). Further, the *Blue Book* discussion is a criticism of the idea that it is the common property which is the justification for applying the general term "game" to the various games (*BB*, p. 17). Wittgenstein is therefore proposing the thesis that a ground for ascribing a concept to an object need not constitute a logically necessary condition for the truth of the proposition that the object falls under the concept. I shall refer to this as the *family resemblance thesis*.

Commentators on this subject have proposed a variety of alternative interpretations. One which has been suggested is that Wittgenstein is claiming that a certain minimum number of characteristics out of a specified set must be present for an object to be classified under a certain concept. This is attributed to Wittgenstein by L. Pompa in his paper, "Family Resemblance", although he agrees with several other writers in regarding it as basically unworkable. However, there is no textual evidence for this suggestion, and no convincing reason has been given as to why Wittgenstein should wish to hold such a curious position. A different kind of interpretation is that given by Michael Simon.[1] He suggests that the members of a conceptual family resemble, and deviate from, a standard or paradigm, and that sufficient resemblance to this paradigm justifies the ascription of the relevant property. Some of Wittgenstein's pronouncements could be interpreted in this manner, for example, the remark that it is primarily the apparatus of our ordinary language that we call "language", and other things are called languages by analogy with this (*PI*, §494; see also *PG*, §73). However, in this case it is unclear what value lies in talking about families. One might interpret Wittgenstein's discussion as concerning ambiguity, as claiming that a word like "game" has a number of different meanings, but he explicitly rejects this in the *Grammatik* (§35): "What we call 'games' are procedures interrelated in various ways with many different transitions between one and another." Another account of family resemblance is that Wittgenstein is suggesting that a concept be given a definition in the form of a disjunction of features possessed by the objects falling under the concept, but this is dismissed in the *Investigations* as "only playing with words" (*PI*, §67). In summary, it is unfortunately the case that previous interpretations of family resemblance have been singularly unilluminating.

One criticism of the family resemblance thesis which has been proposed by Pompa, and also by Hjalmar Wennerberg,[2] is that since any two things resemble each other in some respect, or can be related by a series of "links", the notion of a "family" operative here is vacuous. It is therefore for Wittgenstein to give us a criterion for deciding which resemblances determine membership of the family, and which do not. As he himself remarks: "Mathematics is, then, a family; but that is not to say that we shall not mind what is incorporated into it" (*RFM*, V, § 26). Wennerberg rejects the idea that one can give a definition of which resemblances are family resemblances, but insofar as the rules for the employment of words are laid down by human convention, family resemblances are simply those properties of objects which are conventionally taken to justify the ascription of a concept. That is, one simply has to "look and see" which features are actually used. On the other hand, it has been pointed out that what determines a family is not resemblance but ancestral relationship, that the concept of a family is logically prior to that of a family resemblance, and that it is merely contingent that the members of a family resemble each other.[3] But Wittgenstein was not interested in the genesis of concepts, because this is a scientific study dealing with hypotheses (*PB*, § 15; *PI*, p. 230). Also, on his account, the meaning of a word is determined by its *present* use. His purpose is simply to emphasize the complexity of the resemblances between the items falling under a given concept, the multiplicity of possible justifications, and the metaphor of family resemblance, as indicated previously, might be replaced by any of a series of others.

It has often been claimed that Wittgenstein's discussion offers a solution to the problem of universals.[4] However, W.E. Kennick has criticized this kind of interpretation, following an observation made by Robert J. Richman.[5] It is clear that Wittgenstein is criticising the position that the referents of a general term must have something in common, a position which Richman calls "essentialism". However, he points out that this position does not entail any ontological claim about subsistent essences, though it is historically true that essentialism is often associated with a metaphysical realism. Kennick also argues that the "family resemblance" passages are not directed at realism or nominalism, and he suggests that both realist and non-realist forms of essentialism are to be found in classical texts. I would like to point out, moreover, that it is possible to hold a metaphysical realism without being committed to essentialism, for such a position is to be found in Aristotle's doctrine of equivocals.[6] Things are called "equivocal", Aristotle says, if they are all denoted by the same name, but if the relation between different things and the name is given by different definitions (*Cat.*, I, 1a1-6). One such case is where things are called by the same name because of something to which they all in one way or another have reference (*pros en*) (*E N*, I 6, 1096b23-29). In the *Metaphysics,* Aristotle discusses examples of *pros en* equivocity, notably, things which exist, things which are healthy, and things which are "medical" (Γ 2, 1003a34-b5); *K* 3, 1060b36-1061a7). It transpires from this discussion that the equivocity is expressed in reference to one form, and so the things denoted by the term can be united under one science: in the case of being, the science is philosophy. Aristotle says that things which are equivocal *pros en* have something in common, namely, that to which they have reference; without something in common there can be no science (*K* 3, 1060b31-36).

Terms and definitions may be said to be equivocal and univocal in an extended sense; the equivocity of words is supposed to manifest the equivocity of the things named. The Aristotelian method rests upon the possibility of direct cognition, of direct acquaintance with objects without the intermediary of language. Having noted the mutual resemblances and differences of things (*Top.*, I 15, 106a9-10) by this activity of direct study, we can then examine whether our language and definitions faithfully mirror their equivocities.

Aristotle's sophisticated notion of "having something in

common" is clearly beyond the reach of whatever criticisms are being made in the discussion of family resemblance.[7] He agrees that we should study the resemblances in the employment of words, but only insofar as they reflect the resemblances between objects. He readily admits that the meaning of a word need not be given by some element which is common (in the usual sense) to all the things described by that word (e.g. *E N, loc. cit.*). Any disagreement between Aristotle and Wittgenstein is to be found elsewhere, in the underlying theory of meaning, and not in the discussion of family resemblance. Indeed, the discussion of the previous chapters would suggest that Wittgenstein would be quite opposed to the kind of metaphysical realism propounded by Aristotle. But if the thesis of family resemblance can be given both a realist slant (as in Aristotle) and a non-realist slant (as in Wittgenstein), it is clearly independent of any particular position on the problem of universals. Further, a corollary of this is that any adequate account of Wittgenstein's discussion of family resemblance and its role in his later philosophy must pay due attention to the semantic theory which motivates and underpins the discussion, and this requires the consideration of passages elsewhere in his writings.

One objection to the thesis of family resemblance which Wittgenstein considers is that one might define a concept, not by giving the disjunction of the common properties (a possibility which was mentioned above), but by giving the logical sum of the individual interrelated concepts (*PI,* § 68). So, for example, one might define the concept of number as the logical sum of the concepts of cardinal number, rational number, real number, etc. Or, one might define the concept of game as the logical sum of the concepts of chess, tennis, cricket, etc. Wittgenstein objects to this idea on the ground that it entails that all generic concepts have rigid limits. In ordinary language, he says, concepts need have no strict boundary, because human convention may not have drawn such a boundary. One can stipulate that a concept is to have a strict boundary, but this stipulation may not correspond to actual usage (*BB*, p. 19; *PI*, §§68, 69; cf. *PI*, §120).

This is a criticism of Frege's principle of completeness of definition, which stated that a definition of a concept "must be complete; it must unambiguously determine, as regards any object, whether or not if falls under the concept (whether or not the predicate is truly assertible of it)."[8] Frege expressed this principle metaphorically by saying that if the extension of a concept is represented by an area on a plane, then that area must have a sharp boundary. An area without a sharp boundary-line would not really be an area at all; similarly a concept that is not sharply defined is wrongly termed a concept. In the *Foundations of Arithmetic* (§1), he says that the principle of completeness of definition is part of a general demand for rigour in logic.

In the *Investigations* and elsewhere, Wittgenstein totally rejects this position. He cites Frege explicitly, and criticizes several versions of the principle (*PI*, §§71, 76-77, 88, 99-100). He bluntly denies that an area with vague boundaries cannot be called an area at all, by saying that a gesture in a certain direction may be perfectly communicative, even if it does not demarcate a strictly circumscribed area (*PI*, §71). Using a metaphor of an inexact picture, he claims that in some circumstances inexactitude may be what is required, rather than exactitude (*ibid.*). In the *Blue Book* (p. 27), he says that the Fregean view of definition is "like saying that the light of my reading lamp is no real light at all because it has no sharp boundary." Again, he argues that an activity does not fail to be a game if we cannot give a complete list of rules (*PI*, §§83, 100; *Z*, §440). To think so is to be dazzled by the notion of the ideal and therefore to fail to see the actual use of the word "game" (*PI*, § 100). Finally, he criticizes those who demand a rigour in logic for imposing a requirement of "crystalline purity" upon ordinary language, instead of pursuing a purely descriptive study (*PI*, § 108). Because the ordinary use of a term may have no sharp boundary, any definition we give may be revisable in the light of counter-examples (*PI*, § 82). In this sense, any boundary we draw will be arbitrary (*PB*, § 211; cf. *Moore* I, pp. 9-10). We may draw a boundary for a particular purpose, just as we may construct a fence around an area for a particular reason, but we do not draw boundaries where we do not need them (*PG*, § 73; *PI*, §§ 69, 499). Further, the boundary is entirely relative to the purpose and says nothing essential about the concept which it surrounds (*PB*, § 211).

Several philosophers have seen fit to refer to the kind of concept being discussed here as "vagueness". In order to clarify Wittgenstein's position, it will be useful to examine the extent to which the concepts he considers may be called "vague". An immediate point of note is that Wittgenstein does not use the word "vague" very much. He only employs it in the *Investigations* after he has introduced the idea of a concept having a broad borderline, and then in an indirect quotation from Frege concerning vague areas (§ 71). The second reference concerns vague pictures (§ 77), and it is not until he has started on his general discussion concerning the nature of philosophy that he talks of "our ordinary vague sentences" (§ 98). There are at least four uses of the term in the *Remarks on the Foundations of Mathematics*. He says that "understanding a mathematical proposition" is a very vague concept (IV, § 46); that saying that the propositions of mathematics determine concepts is vague (V, § 35); that the word "concept" is by far too vague (V, § 38); and that "concept" is a vague concept (V, § 49). In *Zettel* (§ 154), Wittgenstein says that sense and reference are vague concepts. In none of these references, save that concerning Frege's theory of language, does the term seem to carry any great theoretical weight. Wittgenstein makes no attempt to clarify in what respect the various concepts are "vague", and one might conclude that these passages are in themselves of little philosophical importance.

He does of course use other terms, such as "exact" and "inexact". In *Zettel* (§438), he says that talk of exactness may be misleading, because although one might choose to relate two concepts by saying that one is exact, the other inexact, in different cases a different relationship will be in question. The criterion of exactness is relative to one's purpose in employing an "exact" concept rather than an "inexact" one. In the *Investigations* (§88), he says that "inexact" has a somewhat pejorative connotation which he wishes to avoid. A possible contrary of "vague" is "strict", but Wittgenstein's use of this latter term is unclear. For example, in the *Blue Book* (p. 27), he says that many words do not have a strict meaning, in the sense that speakers of the language cannot formulate or articulate a description of their use. This sense is obviously distinct from the sense of "strict" in which whether or not a concept is applicable to an object is determinable for all objects. Yet, Wittgenstein then makes the remark quoted previously concerning the light of a reading lamp having no sharp boundary, a remark which is clearly intended to be a criticism of Frege's theory.

In a paper entitled "Vagueness: An Exercise in Logical Analysis", Max Black considers the concept of vagueness, and gives an account which is similar to Wittgenstein's notion of a broad borderline; that is, a vague concept for Black is one where some cases of application are indeterminate. Haig Khatchadourian has suggested that this is not the usual concept of vagueness, and he defines a vague concept as one which is not precise or exact in meaning.[9]

One may note that vagueness in this sense might be
accounted for in terms of disagreement between the members of a linguistic community over the use of a word,
whereas Wittgenstein's discussion at least seems to concern
cases of uncertainty in each individual; or, more precisely,
it follows from the conventionally *agreed* meaning of a
concept to which his remarks apply that not all cases of
application will be decidable. More important, Khatchadourian appears to be considering a situation where the
applicability of a term is uncertain in every case; but if
there are no consistent criteria of application of a term,
it is not clear that it has any genuine connotation at all.
It is true, however, that the term "vagueness" glosses
over the distinction between genuine concepts where some
cases of application are determinate, some indeterminate,
and pseudo-concepts where all cases are indeterminate.
Wittgenstein's interest lies in the former situation; it is
important, he remarks, that besides the possibility of cases
on the borderline, there are also cases where a word is
applied unambiguously, so that there is not uncertainty
about its use in every case (*PG,* §73; cf. his remark at
RFM, IV, §16, on the "solid core to all these glistening
concept-formations" which is "what makes them into
mathematics"). Further, although we may be able to
construct innumerable borderline cases where doubt exists
(*PG,* §73; *Z,* §440), in practice such cases may be restricted. Either they are never raised ("They do not exist
among our applications of language": *Z,* §117), or they
are excluded by empirical regularities: for example, because
of the relative permanence through time of physical
objects, we are not usually in any doubt as to whether a
particular object is to count as a chair (*PI,* §80).

However, the applicability of a term may be uncertain
for one of two reasons. In the case which is more frequently considered in philosophical discussion, the set of
conditions for the term's employment may be determinate,

but it is uncertain whether they apply in some particular case. But a different situation arises if this set of conditions is itself indeterminate: it is uncertain what counts as a ground for the term's employment and what does not. In his *Introduction to Philosophical Analysis* (pp.40-42), John Hospers discusses cases of the first kind where a set of predicates constitutes a continuum. For example, the colour spectrum includes red and orange, and also a region in between them where it is uncertain which colour-name is applicable. In the *Philosophische Bemerkungen* (§211), and in the *Philosophische Grammatik* (pp. 236-240), Wittgenstein considers further examples of this kind. One involves the problem, "How many grains of sand make a heap?" He says that one might stipulate limits, for example, that a heap is any group of more than one hundred grains, and that a group of less than ten grains is not a heap. But, he adds, these limits are purely arbitrary, and tell us nothing about the concept "heap". A brief reference is made to this example in *Zettel* (§392), where he says that "heap of sand" is a concept without sharp boundaries. Another example considered in the *Bemerkungen* and in the *Grammatik* is that of the visual discrimination of the length of various lines or stripes. The problem over deciding when a group of grains constitutes a heap of sand, he says, is the same problem as that of deciding which of a series of stripes of monotonically varying length are still the same length as a particular stripe, and which are different in length. Now, these cases of uncertainty are not produced by an uncertainty about the ground for calling something "red", for example, but by a failure to discriminate with respect to the paradigms for different colour-words (cf. *PB,* §211). Having said that the concept, "heap of sand", does not have sharp boundaries, Wittgenstein asks: "But why isn't one with sharp boundaries used instead of it?—Is the reason to be found in the nature of the heaps? What is the phenomenon whose nature is definitive for our concept?" (*Z*, § 392). The answer has to do with the psychological facts concerning the ability of human beings to discriminate the size, colour, etc., of physical objects.[10]

In his discussion of broad borderlines, however, Wittgenstein is concerned with the second type of indeterminacy. The game is not vague simply because we are unsure as to whether the rules apply to a particular case, but because we are unsure as to which are the rules (*PI*, § 100). Similarly, what is interesting is the possibility of including new *kinds* or *types* of object in the extension of a concept (*PI*, § 23); it is not just the extension of the concept which is uncertain, but the set of properties justifying its application. For example, in the *Grammatik* (§ 70), Wittgenstein talks about the *right* by which we include a new example in a concept's extension. Of course, if we employ completely new justifications, we shall not have extended the concept, but given the term a different sense; what we must do is to use the term by analogy with our earlier employment, taking most of our justifications from the established meaning of the word. It will be seen in the next chapter that a point which Wittgenstein regards as important is that there is no clear distinction between what is to count as a conventionally determined ground for ascribing a property and what merely constitutes an accidental feature. Just before his discussion of family resemblance and broad borderlines in the *Investigations*, he remarks that one might say that the essential thing about a lamp is that it serves to give light; that it is not essential that it is an ornament, for example. But, he adds, there is not always a sharp distinction between essential and inessential (*PI*, § 62). Finally, in the *Blue Book* (p. 19), Wittgenstein remarks that the concept of wishing does not have a sharp boundary because "there is not one definite class of features which characterize all cases of wishing."

Since the set of grounds for the ascription of a concept

may be indefinite, the justification of assertions need not constitute decisive evidence. Indeed, subsequent evidence may fail to support such assertions, or even contradict them (cf. *BB*, p. 145, on the features which are characteristic of a friendly face). Thus the rules for the employment of a word may not supply logically sufficient grounds for either asserting or denying that the word applies in a particular case. The discussion of broad borderlines thus attacks the idea that the sense of a word is to be explained in terms of necessary and sufficient conditions of application. The grounds of a proposition are necessarily good evidence, in that their evidential value is guaranteed by the linguistic conventions which determine the sense of the proposition, but they need not entail the proposition. Nevertheless, some cases of entailment must be permitted, since they clearly exist in ordinary language: some concepts *can* be defined by giving necessary and sufficient conditions of application. With respect to those definitions they do have sharp boundaries. But a philosophy which asserts that sense is determined by the conditions of justifiable employment will require that any logical relation which can be employed in ordinary language be explicable in terms of those conditions. It will further assert that the important relation for the purposes of conceptual analysis will be that between the employment of linguistic expressions and the justification of that employment (cf. *RFM*, Appx. I, § 2).

On the interpretation which I have presented, therefore, Wittgenstein is proposing the thesis that there need be no ground (or set of grounds) for ascribing a concept to an object which constitutes a logically sufficient condition for the truth of the proposition that the object falls under the concept. I shall refer to this as the *broad borderline thesis*.

It is clear that Wittgenstein thinks of the family resemblance thesis and the broad borderline thesis as being closely related. The discussion in the *Investigations* oscillates between the two, and the same example, that of the concept "game", is used in both cases (*PI*, §§ 66, 68). At Section 71, he opposes the explanation of a concept with blurred edges, which consists in giving examples, with the kind of explanation where one expresses that which is common to the examples. Later, he discusses the problems involved in understanding the role of such a concept in ordinary language, and adds: "In such a difficulty always ask yourself: How did we *learn* the meaning of this word . . . ? . . . Then it will be easier for you to see that the word must have a variety of meanings" (*PI*, § 77). Conversely, Wittgenstein asserts that there is no boundary around the family of things resembling each other (*PI*, § 69). Elsewhere, a similar oscillation is to be found. In the *Blue Book* (p. 19), he says that there is not one definite class of features which characterize all cases of wishing, and that it does not have a sharp boundary. But he then proceeds to criticize "the idea that in order to get clear about the meaning of a general term one had to find the common element in all its applications." In *Zettel* (§§ 111-112), he identifies a word which has "a unified employment" with one which has "a smooth contour", and opposes it to a word with a "ragged" contour.

Some philosophers have claimed that this represents a confusion; there is no direct connection between the two ideas, they suggest, and they ought to be carefully distinguished.[11] However, there are two important respects in which they can be related. The first point is that both the discussion of family resemblance and that of broad borderlines are put forward as attacks upon the kind of semantic theory which asserts that the sense of a word is given by those conditions which are individually necessary and jointly sufficient for its ascription. The second is that both discussions can be interpreted (as they have been interpreted here) as exemplifying and resting upon a semantic theory according to which the sense of a word is determined by the set of conditions which justify its ascription. So, although the two theses stated previously may well be independent within a realist philosophy of language, from a constructivist point of view they can be seen as related, though not as equivalent. Finally, the family resemblance thesis asserts that there may be a variety of possible grounds for employing a word, and the broad borderline thesis makes the additional assertion that there is no strict bound on the set of possible grounds; this set consists simply of those conditions which are conventionally taken to justify the ascription of the word. On this interpretation, then, the family resemblance and broad borderline theses are two sides of the same constructivist coin.

That this kind of interpretation is more or less correct, that the discussion of family resemblance and broad borderlines bears directly upon the opposition of realism and constructivism, is supported by some remarks made by Friedrich Waismann. These are given in his book, *Introduction to Mathematical Thinking* (pp. 237-238; cf. p. 245), but were heavily influenced by Wittgenstein's own ideas. Waismann remarks that the individual concepts of number, by which he means "cardinal number", "integer", etc., form a family. He then gives an account of family resemblance which is taken from a manuscript of Wittgenstein's, possibly that from which the *Grammatik* derives. He then says:

> This is also valid of the expressions "arithmetic," "geometry," "calculus," "operation," "proof," "problem," etc. They all designate families of concepts, and it is of little value to start a controversy regarding their exact definition. In wishing to explain the concept of arithmetic we will point to examples and allow the concept to reach as far as the similarity

reaches in these examples. The very openness, non-closure, of these concepts also has its good points, for it gives language the freedom to comprise new discoveries in a known scheme.

These things had to be discussed here because they provide the background for a question which appears again and again to the meditative mind, namely, are the numbers creations of the human mind, or do they have an autonomous kind of being all of their own? *Are they invented* or are they discovered? A person who looks over the foregoing considerations cannot be in doubt as to the answer. If we were to state our view in a brief formula, we would say: the meaning of a symbol follows from its application. The rules of application only *impart* to the symbols their meaning. Thereby, we reject the interpretation that the rules follow from the meanings of the symbols.

This latter point of view was cited as a central thesis of a realist philosophy of language in the previous chapter, and Waismann himself identifies Frege as its "most important representative". Conversely, that the meaning of a word is constituted by its applications and is not something logically prior to them was, of course, given as the cornerstone of constructivism. Waismann is therefore of the opinion that the correct account of mathematical concepts is a constructivist one, and that this is supported by the fact that such concepts display family resemblance.

This leads on to the question whether all concepts exhibit family resemblance. This question can be answered in two ways. The positive aspect of the family resemblance thesis is to be found in the underlying theory of meaning. Insofar as this is intended as a *general* theory of meaning, it applies to all concepts. The negative aspect of the thesis is that the sense of a word need not be explained in terms of necessary and sufficient conditions of application. This might be thought to require a decision criterion for the cases when sense *can* be explained in this way. But, on a constructivist account, no *philosophical* criterion can be given, since this would state an *a priori* truth about language. In fact, the only possible decision criterion is given by the instruction, "Look and see." Nevertheless, in *The Logic of Vagueness*, Gordon Baker suggests two areas in which Wittgenstein makes particular use of these ideas. The first is the set of formal concepts, the second the set of psychological concepts.

In the *Investigations*, of course, the discussion of family resemblance is given as an answer to the criticism that Wittgenstein fails to give the essence of language. His discussion of the concepts of language, of number, and of rule in the *Philosophische Grammatik* (§§ 69-76) appears to suggest that all formal concepts exhibit family resemblance. Examples actually discussed by Wittgenstein in his later writings include the following: "language" (*PG*, §§ 73, 76; *PI*, §§ 65-108; *Z*, §§ 322, 326); "mathematics" (*RFM*, V, § 26; cf. II, §§ 46, 48; III, § 6; IV, § 46); "number" (*PG*, § 73; *PI*, § 68); "sense" and "reference" (*Z*, § 154); "rule" (*PG*, § 73); "proof" (*BB*, pp. 28-29); and "concept" (see above). He also considers the word "*Satz*", which is of course ambiguous between "sentence" and "proposition" (*PG*, §§ 69, 73, 76; *PI*, §§ 108, 135; see also *Moore* III, p. 21). In the previous chapter, it was pointed out that Wittgenstein believed that "meaning" could be explained in several different ways, depending upon one's purpose (cf. also *BB*, pp. 43-44). And in the passage quoted above from his *Introduction to Mathematical Thinking*, Waismann gives a whole range of formal concepts which, he claims, exhibit family resemblance. Within a particular system or calculus, such concepts are determined by the rules of the calculus; there are different concepts corresponding to different calculi, different grammatical structures (*BB*,

p. 19; *PI*, §108). The formal concepts of ordinary language are not clear-cut, however, and it is these concepts which concern us in philosophy (*PG*, §77; *PI*, §108). Wittgenstein distinguishes the broad-borderline concept of a number from the strict concept of a cardinal number, and he says that they are "concepts" in different senses of the word (*PG*, §70).[12] An important consequence of this is that a correct philosophical account of a formal concept in ordinary language is not to be given in terms of a formal calculus (*BB*, p. 25; *PI*, §81). It is interesting to note that the result of the application of this principle to the concept of a valid mathematical proof is given by Michael Dummett as the intuitionistic interpretation of Gödel's theorem.[13] Waismann (*op. cit.*, pp. 101-102) interprets the theorem as showing that there is no formal system in which all arithmetic concepts could be defined, and he remarks that Brouwer was "on the right track" when he thought of "mathematics as essentially a living activity of thought, a series of meaningful constructive steps and *therefore* not contained in a rigid system of formulae." However, Wittgenstein says that his task is not to talk about Gödel's proof, as this would be doing mathematics, not philosophy; his aim is to pass it by (*RFM*, V, §16).

The second area of application of the family resemblance discussion identified by Baker is that of psychological concepts, particularly dispositions and capacities, such as understanding and meaning. It will be remembered that this is the domain of interest of the discussion in the *Philosophische Grammatik*. In *Zettel* (§§111-113), Wittgenstein appears to put forward a general point concerning all psychological concepts. He says that the naive idea that one forms of the word "thinking" "does not correspond to reality at all. We expect a smooth contour and what we get to see is ragged. . . . It is not to be expected of this word that it should have a unified employment; we should rather expect the opposite." He then adds: "That can of course be said of all psychological verbs. Their employment is not so clear or so easy to get a synoptic view of, as that of terms in mechanics, for example." Subsequently he discusses the corrigibility of the ascription of psychological concepts to others: "The 'uncertainty' relates not to the particular case, but to the method, to the rules of evidence. The uncertainty is not founded on the fact that he does not wear his pain on his sleeve. And there is not an uncertainty *in each particular case*. If the frontier between two counties were in dispute, would it follow that the county to which any individual resident belonged was dubious?" (*Z*, §§ 555-556). So the corrigibility of the ascription of such concepts is built into the linguistic rules determining what counts as a justification for such ascription. Further, the metaphor of the disputed frontier suggests that this corrigibility is not different in kind from the corrigibility attaching to other concepts such as "game". This point will be elaborated in the next chapter.

Within the class of psychological concepts, Wittgenstein differentiates several sub-classes. An important distinction is that between states of consciousness and dispositions or capacities. In later works, such as the *Investigations* and *Zettel*, he tends to make this distinction by pointing out that the former are related to some manifestation throughout an interval of time, whereas capacities do not have to be continuously manifested; however, the latter may be ascertained by spot-checks (*PI*, p. 59; *Z*, § 72). He says that there is a "category-difference" between the two classes of concept (*Z*, § 86). In the *Blue Book* (p. 20), however, he suggests that "a great many different activities and states of mind" may be characteristic of a disposition or capacity, but that there is no single factor in common to all of them, and *a fortiori* there is no one process or state of mind with which a disposition or capacity is to be identified. This idea does occur in the *Investigations* (§ 154), where he says that "in the sense in which there are processes (including mental processes) which are characteristic of understanding, understanding is not a mental process." Later, he says that we must be on our guard against thinking that there is some totality of conditions for a person's possessing a capacity (*PI*, § 183).

Wittgenstein mentions a range of dispositions and capacities, including "understanding", "thinking", "knowing", "believing", "wishing", "intending", "expecting", "meaning", and all cases of volition (*BB*, pp. 19, 20-21, 124-125, 144-145, 150-155; *PG*, § 35; *PI*, §§ 146-156). He draws several negative consequences from the premises that understanding, knowing, and meaning are capacities, and that there is no occurrence, state, or process which is common to all instances of a capacity. For example, if meaning is not a state, it is not a mental state, and hence not an unconscious mental state (*BB*, pp. 113, 152; *PG*, §§ 10, 34-35). If it is not a process, it is not a mental process (*BB*, p. 34; *PI*, § 153; *Z*, § 236), but neither is it a physical or physiological process (*PI*, §§ 157-158). Nor is meaning to be identified with an activity, mental or otherwise (*Z*, § 20). Finally, the meaning of a word is not to be identified with anything that may appear before the mind of the speaker, a mental image, for example (*BB*, p. 65; *PG*, § 13; *PI*, pp. 175-176).

The relevance of these points to the philosophy of language is that for Wittgenstein the possession of a concept, the understanding of a rule, are *capacities* (*Z*, § 421; see also *PG*, §§ 10, 34; *PI*, § 150). Because terms denoting capacities exhibit family resemblance, Wittgenstein criticizes at least three philosophical positions. The first is the idea that there are "certain definite mental processes bound up with the working of language, processes through which alone language can function" (*BB*, p. 3).[14] The second is that the understanding of a rule consists in a mental state which is the source of the correct application of the rule (*PI*, § 146). And the third is the idea that mental occurrences, states, etc., are ever relevant to a philosophy of language. It is the practice of the game that is important, not the mental occurrences of the players (*BB*, p. 65; *PG*, p. 295; *PI*, §680; *RFM*, II, §25). This in turn leads back to the original idea that the meaning of a word is given by its use. For the possession of a concept is to be explained, ascribed, justified, etc., in just the same way as any other capacity, namely, by correct performance (cf. *BB*, pp. 113-117). To possess a concept is to be master of a technique (*PI*, §150).

Another set of concepts which is alleged to exhibit family resemblance might be loosely termed "human actions". These include "deriving", "reading", "recognizing", and "comparing" (*BB*, pp. 85-88, 124-125; *PI*, §§156, 164). However, as the heterogeneity of these examples might suggest, the applicability of the family resemblance thesis cuts across any categorization. Formal concepts, such as "proposition", are said to be analogous to "game" and "plant" (*PG*, §73; *PI*, §135). Wittgenstein remarks that "the concept of a living being has the same indeterminacy as that of a language" (*Z*, §326), and that "the use of the words 'proposition', 'language', etc. has the haziness of the normal use of concept-words in our language" (*PG*, §76; cf. *PI*, §97). In the *Grammatik*, it will be recalled, the word "game" was supposed to illustrate the behaviour of a whole range of dispositions and capacities (*PG*, §35). Elsewhere in that work, he assimilates the concepts of "proposition" and "experience" (§70), and he says that "thought" and "language" are "fluid" concepts (§65). As a quite different example of the applicability of the theses of family resemblance and broad borderlines, Wittgenstein asserts without argument that "goodness" has a family of meanings and a blurred boundary, and he intimates that this is the case with all concepts of ethics and aesthetics (*PI*, §77; see also *PG*, §36). If these remarks are considered against the background of the discussion so far, it would appear that Wittgenstein's constructivism extends (as it should to be consistent) to an ethical relativism.

The term "family resemblance" tends to be scattered liberally about philosophical writings, though usually without any explanation of what is meant by the phrase. J.J. Katz remarks that it is usually left entirely unexplained or else described in terms of some quite unilluminating analogy, although he himself attempts to give some exegesis of Wittgenstein's use of the term (*The Philosophy of Language*, pp. 71-76, 95). In all of the passages in Wittgenstein's writings where it is employed, it is quite clear what position he is attacking; namely, the doctrine that the meaning of a word is to be given in terms of those conditions which are individually necessary and jointly sufficient for its correct application. However, on what grounds he makes this attack, and what he wishes to propose as an alternative semantic theory, is by no means obvious from the immediate context, though I have suggested that there are some hints. However, it is of course quite unreasonable to expect to grasp an author's position by confining one's attention to a few paragraphs, although this has been the strategy of all too many of Wittgenstein's commentators and critics. A semantic theory can be derived from other passages, as I hope by this time to have shown, and the discussion of family resemblance can make at least a reasonable sense when seen against the background of this theory. Positively, it has little to add directly to the theory of meaning, although it produces some interesting corollaries; yet it does serve to bring out an important negative consequence of that theory. This consequence, however, is only negative with respect to traditional conceptions of meaning; within Wittgenstein's theory it is simply a feature of the "grammar of justification".

I hope to have shown what relationship exists between

the discussion of family resemblance and that of broad borderlines. They do appear to be discussing distinct criticisms of the traditional theory of meaning. They do not appear to establish theses with any logical relations between each other. (It is true that the truth of p is a necessary condition of the truth of q, if, and only if, the truth of q is a sufficient condition of the truth of p; but if p is one of the circumstances conventionally justifying the assertion of q, and hence one of the circumstances constituting the *meaning* of q, q cannot stand in any such relation to p.) However, the two theses which I have identified are complementary attacks on the traditional point of view, and both are consequences of the theory of meaning elaborated earlier. Thus, there is every reason why Wittgenstein should wish to discuss them together. I hope also to have removed some misconceptions about the content and subject-matter of these discussions. The discussion of family resemblance does not have to do with the "problem" of universals, although the underlying theory of meaning does have consequences in that direction. The discussion of broad borderlines is not about vagueness, nor is it about the kind of "marginal indeterminacy" which prevents us from being certain about all applications of colour concepts, for example (though this problem is discussed elsewhere in Wittgenstein's writings).

Finally, Wittgenstein does mention some interesting consequences of his two theses. One is that one cannot give an adequate account of a formal concept (such as "proposition", "proof", and "number") in terms of a formal calculus. This gives a general version of the consequence which some philosophers would wish to draw from Godel's theorem, but it does so on philosophical, rather than mathematical, grounds. Another consequence is a direct attack on psychologistic theories of meaning. In the discussions considered in previous chapters, Wittgenstein appeared to be happy to allow alternative conceptions of meaning for purposes other than his own. However, in at least two of his discussions of family resemblance, and in several other passages, he gives the general argument that human dispositions and capacities are not to be identified with mental states, processes, or occurrences, and he draws the particular consequence of this view that meaning and understanding are not to be explained in this way. In one sense this simply reiterates his basic conception of language, as a set of techniques. But it also puts forward a philosophical position which is important in its own right.

Chapter V

THE THEORY OF CRITERIA

A topic of discussion in the study of Wittgenstein's writings which has received particular attention in recent years is his concept of a "criterion". This term is associated especially with the problem of our knowledge of other minds, but Wittgenstein's remarks also have important consequences for the philosophy of language. In this chapter, I would like to consider what Wittgenstein has to say concerning criteria, and to compare this with various points which have already arisen in the discussion of his later theory of meaning. It will be seen that the two kinds of discussion have many shared themes, and that, far from being an isolated though important topic in the philosophy of mind, the theory of criteria also takes an integral position in Wittgenstein's semantic theory.

In the *Blue Book* (pp. 23-24), Wittgenstein suggests that a way of examining the grammar or use of a word is to consider what is the case when sentences containing the word are used to make true statements:

> It is part of the grammar of the word "chair" that *this* is what we call "to sit on a chair", and it is part of the grammar of the word "meaning" that *this* is what we call "explanation of a meaning"; in the same way to explain my criterion for another person's having toothache is to give a grammatical explanation about the word "toothache" and, in this sense, an explanation concerning the meaning of the word "toothache".

So an explanation of the grammar of "toothache" might

involve specifying what must be the case for one to say of a person that he has toothache. That which is used in order to ascribe toothache is called a *criterion.* Wittgenstein explains what kind of thing he has in mind:

> When we learnt the use of the phrase "so-and-so has toothache" we were pointed out certain kinds of behaviour of those who were said to have toothache. As an instance of these kinds of behaviour let us take holding your cheek. Suppose that by observation I found that in certain cases whenever these first criteria told me a person had toothache, a red patch appeared on the person's cheek. Supposing I now said to someone "I see A has toothache, he's got a red patch on his cheek". He may ask me "How do you know A has toothache when you see a red patch?" I shall then point out that certain phenomena had always coincided with the appearance of the red patch.

The ascription of toothache on the basis of one kind of evidence *E* can thus be justified by citing some other evidence *E'* which has been observed to regularly coincide with *E.* However, certain kinds of behaviour are cited as being characteristic of toothache when the word "toothache" is taught. In fact, it appears to be its involvement in such teaching which gives this latter evidence a more fundamental status, such that it can indeed justify the ascription of toothache on the basis of different kinds of evidence.

> Now one may go on and ask: "How do you know that he has got toothache when he holds his cheek?" The answer to this might be, "I say, *he* has toothache when he holds his cheek because I hold my cheek when I have toothache." But what if we went on asking:—"And why do you suppose that toothache corresponds to his holding his cheek just because your

toothache corresponds to your holding your cheek?"
You will be at a loss to answer this question, and find
that here we strike rock bottom, that is we have come
down to conventions.

Thus the evidential value of those evidences which Wittgenstein calls "criteria" is guaranteed by linguistic convention. This also appears in a passage later on in the *Blue
Book*:

> The man who says "only my pain is real", doesn't
> mean to say that he has found out by the common
> criteria—the criteria, i.e., which give our words their
> common meaning—that the others who said they had
> pains were cheating. But what he rebels against is the
> use of *this* expression in connection with *these* criteria.
> That is, he objects to using this word in the particular
> way in which it is commonly used. On the other hand,
> he is not aware that he is objecting to a convention
> (p. 57).

So the criteria for pain are those behavioural characteristics which are conventionally taken to justify the
ascription of pain. On the other hand, the evidential
value of the other kinds of evidence which might
be employed to justify the ascription of pain is guaranteed merely by the empirical fact that they regularly
coincide with the criteria of pain.

To explain this distinction, Wittgenstein introduces the
metaphor of diagnosing an illness (*BB*, pp. 24-25). A diagnosis might be justified non-inductively by pointing to the
phenomenon which is the "defining criterion" of the illness, or it might be justified inductively by pointing to a
"symptom", a phenomenon which has been observed to
regularly coincide with the criterion. For example, one
might justify the diagnosis of angina either by identifying a

particular bacillus in the patient's blood, or by observing an inflammation of the throat. Now, this passage has given rise to some degree of confusion and controversy. In a recent paper on "Symptoms", Jerry S. Clegg has given a perceptive account of the role of symptoms in clinical diagnosis, and has indicated the implications of his account for the interpretation of this passage from the *Blue Book*. First, he argues that a symptom is not merely a sign of an ailment. It is true that a symptom of a tumour might be regarded as a sign of a tumour, but a tumour is not in itself an ailment (though it may be the cause of certain ailments). Similarly, a bacillus in the bloodstream may cause distressing symptoms, but is not itself constitutive of an ailment. Generally speaking, it is the symptoms which are constitutive of an ailment. In fact, Clegg points out, if one has no symptoms, one is not ill; one may have a bacillus, but one is then a carrier of the disease, not its victim. Second, while symptoms are used to justify diagnoses, they are not usually either necessary or sufficient conditions of the disease of which they are symptomatic. Further, they may be ambiguous, so that the same symptom or set of symptoms may be symptomatic of several different ailments. In such a case, some phenomenon is required which removes the ambiguity. Such a phenomenon will be discovered to be empirically correlated with the set of symptoms which constitute the disease, and may consist, for example, in the result of a chemical analysis of the patient's urine, or in the discovery of a bacillus. Such tests are causally related to the disease and are in no way constitutive of it; they merely serve to identify the disease. Such tests and causal agents Clegg refers to as "criteria". However, even criteria are not necessary or sufficient conditions. They are not sufficient, because the patient may be merely a carrier of the disease; they are not necessary, because the empirical correlation between symptoms and criteria may fail. Nevertheless, criteria may be useful

109

aids towards arriving at the correct diagnosis.

Clegg then proceeds to argue that Wittgenstein's discussion on pages 24 and 25 of the *Blue Book* is directly in accord with this account. He points out that Wittgenstein suggests as a definition of angina, "an inflammation caused by a particular bacillus", and therefore concludes that for Wittgenstein the inflammation which is symptomatic of angina is actually constitutive of the disease. The bacillus which is given as the criterion of angina cannot be completely constitutive of the disease, as this would fail to distinguish carriers from victims. So, although the criteria affect usage and meaning, they do not completely determine the use of a disease term. Nevertheless, apart from the *a priori* implausibility of maintaining that virtually all of Wittgenstein's interpreters are, as it were, out of step, it is easy to show that this account of his ideas is incorrect. A more detailed account of the distinction between criteria and symptoms will be given later in this chapter, but certain relevant comments can be made on the basis of the discussion so far. For Wittgenstein, the important distinction is that between evidences which are learned as being characteristic of an occurrence (e.g. toothache), and evidences which are subsequently discovered to be correlated with the first kind. The former are established by linguistic convention, and these have already been defined as "criteria" before the opposition between criteria and symptoms is mentioned (*BB*, p. 24). The latter kind of evidence, however, is entirely parasitic upon the former for its evidential value. Further, Wittgenstein does not necessarily wish criteria and symptoms to stand in the kind of causal relationship which Clegg describes. Indeed, he wishes to say that in practice it may be difficult to tell which phenomena are criteria and which symptoms. Subsequently, in the *Brown Book* (p. 113), he criticizes the use of the word "symptom" in the case of human capacities since it may mislead one into thinking that there exists one particular activity, process, or state "which is somehow hidden from our eyes but manifests itself in those occurrents which we call symptoms (as an inflammation of the mucous membranes of the nose produces the symptom of sneezing)." Nevertheless, he is drawing the same distinction here as in the earlier passage. For he distinguishes actual demonstrations of the capacity (which logically justify its ascription), from other behaviour which is empirically correlated with the possession of the capacity; for example, uttering a mathematical formula which correctly describes a series of numbers, as opposed to actually continuing the series. In this sense we can say that uttering the formula is only a symptom of the capacity.

Now, the reason why Clegg attributes to Wittgenstein the thesis that criteria are not entirely constitutive of that for which they are criteria, is that, as he points out, the opposite position, that symptoms are empirically associated with that of which they are symptomatic, cannot account for the difference between the carrier and the victim of a disease. The appropriate resolution of this difficulty appears to be that of retaining the interpretation offered previously of the notion of a criterion (an interpretation to be bolstered by further argument), but to admit that this does not give the correct account of medical diagnosis. More precisely, Wittgenstein ought to have acknowledged that *medical* symptoms function as *logical* criteria. Once again, however, the situation of clinical diagnosis is clearly intended only as a metaphor (the passage is given as a philosophical discussion of "toothache", not of "angina"), one with which Wittgenstein himself was clearly not completely satisfied. In support of this account, it is useful to consider how Wittgenstein elaborates the distinction between criteria and symptoms:

> If medical science calls angina an inflammation caused
> by a particular bacillus, and we ask in a particular case

"why do you say this man has got angina?" then the
answer "I have found the bacillus so-and-so in his
blood" gives us the criterion, or what one may call
the defining criterion of angina. If on the other hand
the answer was, "His throat is inflamed", this might
give us a symptom of angina. I call "symptom" a
phenomenon of which experience has taught us that
it coincided, in some way or another, with the phenomenon which is our defining criterion. Then to say
"A man has angina if this bacillus is found in him"
is a tautology or it is a loose way of stating the
definition of "angina". But to say, "A man has angina
whenever he has an inflamed throat" is to make a
hypothesis (*BB*, p. 25).

The use of the words "tautology", "definition", and
"hypothesis" clearly suggests that Wittgenstein is opposing
a logical relation to an empirical relation, consistent with
the interpretation which has been given so far.

However, the use of these terms has also suggested to
many commentators that the criterial relationship described
in the passage quoted above is a somewhat strict logical
relation, to be assimilated perhaps to entailment. One of
the first writers to suggest this was Rogers Albritton, in
his paper, "On Wittgenstein's Use of the Term 'Criterion'."
With reference to pages 24 and 25 of the *Blue Book*, he
concludes: "It is plain enough, then, though Wittgenstein
might have made it plainer, that in the sense of the passages
I've quoted from the *Blue Book* the criterion for this or
that's being so is, among other things, a logically sufficient
condition of its being so. That is: If I find in a particular
case that the criterion for a thing's being so is satisfied,
what entitles me to claim that I thereby know the thing
to be so is that the satisfaction of the criterion *entails* that
it is so, in the technical sense of 'entails' in which if a man
owns two suitcases, that entails that he owns some luggage."

However, Albritton also suggests that the *Blue Book* conception of a criterion was "almost entirely suppressed" in later writings such as the *Investigations*. He suggests an alternative conception in the *Blue Book* itself, such that the criteria for the truth of a proposition are evidences for the proposition (cf. *BB*, pp. 51-52), and cites this as the "dominant conception" of the later writings. Anthony Kenny offers a similar account (in his article, "Criterion"). He remarks: "One conclusion which we might draw from this passage [*BB*, pp. 24-25] is that a criterion differs from a symptom in being a decisive piece of evidence." However, he also suggests that Albritton's account is "certainly wrong" as an exegesis of the *Philosophical Investigations,* and suggests that this latter work employs a notion which is to be identified with that of "non-inductive evidence". Finally, in a recent work, P.M.S. Hacker argues that the relevant passage from the *Blue Book* (p. 25) "is misleading. It clearly suggests that a criterion is a sufficient condition or even a necessary and sufficient condition. It is quickly noted that this concept of a defining, decisive criterion is at odds with the notion of a criterion at work in the *Investigations*. However it is equally obvious that Wittgenstein's extensive employment of 'criterion' in the second half of the *Blue Book* no more coincides with this first explanation than does his usage in later works."[1]

However, there are several reasons for regarding this commonly accepted account of page 25 of the *Blue Book* as being quite mistaken, aside from the obvious implausibility of holding that Wittgenstein referred to two contradictory notions by the same technical term in the same work. First, as Kenny points out, it follows from Albritton's account that on the *Blue Book* conception there can only be a single criterion for a given state of affairs. Yet, immediately before the discussion of criteria and symptoms, Wittgenstein talks of the criteria for toothache, the various kinds of behaviour characteristic of those who are said to have toothache. Holding one's cheek is but one instance of these kinds of behaviour (*BB*, p. 24). Second, an account which identifies "criterion" with "sufficient condition" is committed to a behaviourist interpretation of Wittgenstein's philosophy of mind, but there is very little independent evidence for such an interpretation, especially in the *Blue Book*. Third, Wittgenstein had previously criticized the dependence upon entailment in conceptual analysis in a statement of the family resemblance and broad borderline theses (*BB*, pp. 17-20), and he immediately proceeds to attack the idea that language is used according to strict rules (*BB*, p. 25) and that words must have a strict meaning (*BB*, pp. 27-28). Fourth, Wittgenstein's supposed "extensive employment" of the term in the second half of the *Blue Book* in fact amounts to no more than half a dozen occurrences, the clearest of which (p. 57) is quoted above and is entirely consistent with the early passages (e.g. p. 24). Finally, to identify "defining criterion" with "decisive evidence" presupposes that those phenomena which are cited in an explanation of a term are sufficient conditions of the term's application. Hence the common account of the *Blue Book* idea of a criterion rests upon a principle which Wittgenstein himself rejected. There is indeed a conceptual relation here, in that those phenomena which are pointed out as characteristic of toothache, for example, are subsequently used to justify the ascription of toothache, and their evidential value is guaranteed by the conventions which are constituted by such occasions of teaching and application. So, if p is a criterion for q, it is a necessary truth that p is evidence for q. But none of this suggests that p would entail q, and to suppose otherwise, Wittgenstein would suggest, is to fall victim to a dogma.

As will be seen in a moment, it is perhaps the case that there are some changes in what is taken to count as a criterion for what in Wittgenstein's later writings. But there are no important changes, from the *Blue Book* onwards, in

what constitutes a criterion, though this must be spelled
out in more detail. One might agree with Hacker, though,
in regarding the discussion of criteria and symptoms on page
25 of the *Blue Book* as "misleading". Indeed, it has been
shown to be misleading on two different counts: it offered
an incorrect account of medical diagnosis, and it tended
to disguise, rather than exhibit, Wittgenstein's actual position on the status of criteria. It is thus no wonder that no
similar discussion of medical diagnosis occurs elsewhere in
Wittgenstein's later writings, and that the whole metaphor
is soon regarded by him as misleading.

It will be useful, at this juncture, to recapitulate the
various points which can be derived from the passage on
pages 24 and 25 of the *Blue Book*. The purpose of this
passage is to elaborate the technical term "criterion" as
applied to the word "toothache". The criteria of toothache
are established by linguistic convention, and they determine
the meaning of "toothache". On the other hand, the
symptoms of toothache are discovered in experience, and
do not contribute to the meaning of "toothache". It is
clear from the quotations given earlier that the criteria of
toothache are among the circumstances which are conventionally regarded as appropriate for the ascription of "toothache", and so this discussion exemplifies the theory of
meaning which has been elaborated in the previous chapters of this essay. Further, as has already been pointed
out, "criteria" and "symptoms" are introduced as different
kinds of justification for assertions: they are given in
answer to the question, "How do you know that so-and-so
is the case?" (*BB*, pp. 24-25).

Apart from the passages already mentioned, there are a
few other instances in the *Blue Book* where the term
"criterion" is used. Wittgenstein talks of the criteria of
identity of physical objects and the criteria of identity of
persons (pp. 55, 61). However, in neither of these cases is

it clear that the term is supposed to carry any special weight. He also talks of the criteria for the localization of pains, but again without any elaboration (p. 49). However, there is one important discussion where Wittgenstein appears to make the general point that assertions concerning physical objects are justified by descriptions of subjective experience (pp. 51-53). Here, he refers to particular experiences, or descriptions of such experiences, as "criteria", and he remarks:

> The grammar of propositions which we call propositions about physical objects admits of a variety of evidences for every such proposition. It characterizes the grammar of the proposition "my finger moves, etc." that I regard the propositions "I see it move", "I feel it move", "He sees it move", "He tells me that it moves" etc. as evidences for it.

It is this passage which is cited by Albritton and Hacker as exhibiting a different concept of "criterion" from that described on page 25 of the *Blue Book*. But, apart from the fact that the sorts of term connected by the criterial relation are different, there appears to be no foundation for this claim. I have already criticized the account given by these authors of the earlier passage, and it is this mistaken account which is given as evidence for their claim. In addition, it is evident that several features of the concept of a criterion which have already been identified are present in this passage. For example, the relation is clearly one of evidence for assertions. Further, the value of this evidence rests upon the meanings of the propositions justified. And the use of the expression, "I regard", suggests that these meanings are established by conventions which I choose to follow. With reference to the previous passage, it was pointed out that the criterial relation would be less than strict entailment, for otherwise Wittgenstein would be committed to a behaviourist account of psychological concepts. In the case of evidence for propositions about physical objects, as was observed in Chapter III, he points out that appearances may be deceptive, and one set of evidence may be controverted by another set. So, in this discussion, too, the criterial relation is weaker than entailment.

One might therefore suggest that Wittgenstein has in mind (at least) three classes of proposition, concerning subjective experience, physical objects, and the psychological states of others, respectively; and that there are logical relationships between these three classes, such that the first kind counts as evidence for the second, and the second counts as evidence for the third. That is, one might ascribe to Wittgenstein the view that language is *stratified.* In his thesis, *The Logic of Vagueness,* Gordon P. Baker has given the evidence for this kind of account of the theory of criteria. The evidence is mainly historical, consisting chiefly in a series of papers published by Friedrich Waismann around 1945-1946, which had been written in co-operation with Wittgenstein during the early 1930s and which had originally been intended as expositions of the latter's ideas.[2] Waismann explains his conception of language as follows: "We may set ourselves the task of grouping statements of our language according to the similarity of their usage in distinct domains, in *language-strata* as I shall venture to call them. Thus laws [of nature] will form one language stratum, material object statements another one, sense datum statements yet another one, and so on." However, although it is highly probable that a thesis concerning language-strata might have been held by Wittgenstein at some stage in his philosophizing (most likely around 1930), there is very little direct textual evidence to support this idea, or the further claim that the theory of criteria has its origins in such a thesis. As I have indicated, the period for which the latter claim might most plausibly be made is that of the *Blue Book,* but there are some difficulties even here. For example, Wittgenstein explains the terms "criteria" and "symptoms" by reference to angina, without indicating that justifying the ascription of pain is in any important respect different from the justification of a diagnosis; yet here symptoms and illness are in the same stratum, the domain of physical objects. Further, it is surprising that he apparently cites "He sees it move" as a justification that I can use to support the assertion, "my finger moves", if this passage (p. 51) is only supposed to concern subjective experience. It is true that in the *Blue Book* he discusses the problem of mind and matter, and argues that the difference is not one of different kinds of objects or phenomena, but one of grammar (pp. 47-49). However, here he conflates subjective experience and the psychological states of others, and does not discuss differences in evidential relations. On the language-strata conception, it would be the height of folly to confound two distinct strata in this manner. But, even if one interprets the remarks on pages 51-53 as arguing that statements concerning physical objects are to be justified by descriptions of subjective experience, there is ample evidence that Wittgenstein rejected this position in later writings. And the reason for denying that descriptions of subjective experience can justify one's assertions is the fundamental point that justification must be public and shareable. The language of sense-impressions, like any other, is founded upon public convention (*PI*, § 355). Of course, I may know that something is coloured red because I see that it is red; but I can only justify my ascription of the predicate "red" to that object by showing that I know what "red" means, namely, by pointing to a sample.[3]

It is not until after the *Blue Book* that Wittgenstein manages to give a developed account of psychological concepts. But all of his subsequent writings agree in identifying at least a central class of such concepts by an asymmetry between the first and third persons in their present-tense use: their ascription to others is to be justified by reference to behavioural criteria, their ascription to oneself is not (e.g. *NL*, pp. 277, 278, 281, 284; *PI*, §§ 289, 290, 377, 404; *Z*, §§ 472 ff.). So there is not a case of a peculiar evidential relation, which would be required by the stratification point of view, but one where evidence is not required in certain uses. It can therefore be concluded that even if Wittgenstein held a theory of language-strata at some stage in his philosophizing, and even if such a theory underlies the conception of a criterion in the *Blue Book* (which is at least questionable), such an interpretation is unlikely to be useful for an adequate understanding of the development of this concept in his later philosophy. The most that can be said is that the criterial relation defines a partial ordering on propositions in terms of their logical and epistemological interdependencies.

Indeed, even in the *Philosophische Grammatik*—a work which was written before the dictation of the *Blue Book*—Wittgenstein employs the term "criterion" for a different domain, that of human capacities. It is to be noted that this class of concepts does not exhibit a first/third person asymmetry. He says that what one counts as the criterion for saying that one can do something will show the sense in which one is using the word "can" (*PG*, § 10). He suggests as alternative criteria of understanding a rule either the ability to recite the verbal expression of the rule, or satisfactory performance in tests of being able to apply the rule. In fact, he remarks, we consider the statement of the rule as a symptom for being able to do something other than simply stating a rule. In the same way, the fact that a watch ticks does not lead us to expect simply that it will continue to tick, but also that it will continue to tell us the right time (*PG*, § 42). Although it is not made explicit, the distinction made here between criteria and symptoms again appears to be a distinction between a logical relation and an empirical relation. For it is surely an empirical fact that

119

a watch will usually tell the right time if it is still ticking, whereas the criteria for an ability contribute to the sense of the term describing the ability, and to the sense of statements ascribing that ability.

Subsequently, in the *Investigations*, Wittgenstein says that the criteria which demonstrate the possession of a capacity are different from the criteria which justify the ascription of mental states or processes, and hence understanding, for example, is not to be identified with any "inner process" (*PI*, p. 181). So, although there is a different kind of evidence in the case of capacities from that in the case of mental states, the relation between the evidence and the thing evidenced, the criterial relation, appears to be the same in the two cases. However, because justification must be public, capacities, like states, are to be ascribed on the basis of characteristic behaviour: "Let us remember that there are certain criteria in a man's behaviour for the fact that he does not understand a word: that it means nothing to him, that he can do nothing with it. And criteria for his 'thinking he understands', attaching some meaning to the word, but not the right one. And, lastly, criteria for his understanding the word right" (*PI*, § 269). He relates capacities of human beings to dispositions of objects (e.g. the fact that a cylinder *C* will fit into a hollow cylinder *H*), and remarks: "The criteria which we accept for 'fitting', 'being able to', 'understanding', are much more complicated than might appear at first sight" (*PI*, § 182). In the *Brown Book* (pp. 101-104), he points out that the ascription of a disposition to an object, or of a capacity to a human being, is justified by certain tests; these tests he calls "defining criteria". Finally, he considers the criteria for human dispositions: "Expectation is, grammatically, a state; like: being of an opinion, hoping for something, knowing something, being able to do something. But in order to understand the grammar of these states it is necessary to ask: 'What counts as a criterion for anyone's being in such a state?' (States of hardness, of weight, of fitting)" (*PI*, §572). There is thus no foundation for the claim that the criterial relation is peculiar to psychological concepts. Further, the fact that Wittgenstein extends it even to dispositional properties of objects suggests that it is of potentially general application.[4]

Under the assumption that the realm of discourse to which the term "criterion" is applied is largely unimportant, I shall consider in more detail what Wittgenstein has to say concerning this semantic relation. In his "Notes for Lectures on 'Private Experience' and 'Sense Data'," he develops the *Blue Book* discussion of the employment of psychological concepts. He says that there is behaviour which is characteristic of showing one's toothache, and, on the other hand, there is behaviour which is characteristic of hiding one's toothache (p. 290). Further,

> It is clear that we in our language use the words "seeing red" in such a way that we can say "A sees red but doesn't show it"; on the other hand it is easy to see that we should have no use for these words if their application was severed from the criteria of behaviour. That is to say: to the language game which we play with these words it is both essential that the people who play it behave in the particular way.we call expressing (saying, showing) what they see, and also that sometimes they more or less entirely conceal what they see (p. 286).

These criteria are among the rules of our common language (p. 293). The passage just quoted also includes the point mentioned in Chapter III that language-games are activities comprising systems of rules which determine what constitutes adequate justification (in this case the appropriate behaviour) for the ascription of a concept (in this case "seeing red"). These ideas are elaborated in later writings.

Wittgenstein says that psychological concepts require criteria for the correctness of their application (*PI*, §§ 56, 258). These criteria must be public: the use of a term must be institutionalized. Hence such concepts are to be ascribed on the basis of a characteristic behavioural manifestation (*PI*, § 377), or, as Wittgenstein expresses it: "An 'inner process' stands in need of outward criteria" (*PI*, § 580). Without behavioural criteria psychological concepts would be unusable (*Z*, § 571). Consequently such concepts are applicable to other species only insofar as they resemble human beings in their appearance and behaviour (*PI*, §§ 281, 283).

In the *Brown Book* (pp. 143-144), Wittgenstein discusses the ascription of belief by analogy with the notion of a change in a person's taste in designing a particular kind of object. He remarks that although one might cite the production of a new style as a criterion for a change in taste, it is perfectly possible that someone could produce a new design without having changed their taste. Similarly, the fact that someone says that he believes something might be a criterion for saying that he does believe it, yet it is quite possible for someone to say he believes something without believing it. So, once again, the criterial relation is an evidential relation, but is something weaker than entailment.

The distinction between criteria and symptoms recurs at several points. In the *Investigations* (§ 79), Wittgenstein distinguishes between the observed concomitants of a scientific phenomenon and its defining characteristics. In *Zettel* (§§ 438-439), the two terms are related to that evidence which offers sufficient justification and that which does not. One might note that the term "sufficient" is ambiguous between "logically adequate" (i.e. failing any counter-evidence) and "logically decisive". For an investigation of the grammar of psychological concepts, only the "logical criteria" are relevant, not the symptoms (*Z*, § 466).

When this distinction is introduced in the *Blue Book* (p. 25), Wittgenstein points out that there is frequently some uncertainty concerning which features are to be categorized as criteria and which as symptoms:

> In practice, if you were asked which phenomenon is the defining criterion and which is a symptom, you would in most cases be unable to answer this question except by making an arbitrary decision *ad hoc*. It may be practical to define a word by taking one phenomenon as the defining criterion, but we shall easily be persuaded to define the word by means of what, according to our first use, was a symptom. Doctors will use names of diseases without ever deciding which phenomena are to be taken as criteria and which as symptoms; and this need not be a deplorable lack of clarity. For remember that in general we don't use language according to strict rules—it hasn't been taught us by means of strict rules, either.

He says that there may be no definite borderline between what counts as sufficient evidence and what does not (Z, §439). However, the fact that criteria and symptoms are not always sharply differentiated does not prevent them from being differentiated (Z, §466). Further, as intimated in the quotation above, Wittgenstein believes that there is a continuous fluctuation in the grammar of a language between whether a phenomenon counts as a criterion and whether it counts as a symptom (*PI*, §354).

Now, all of these remarks are supposed to apply equally well to scientific definitions. The example of the criterion for a disease has already been well discussed. In *Zettel* (§438), Wittgenstein makes the following remark:

> Nothing is commoner than for the meaning of an expression to oscillate, for a phenomenon to be regarded sometimes as a symptom, sometimes as a

criterion, of a state of affairs. And mostly in such a case the shift of meaning is not noted. In science it is usual to make phenomena that allow of exact measurement into defining criteria for an expression; and then one is inclined to think that now the proper meaning has been *found.* Innumerable confusions have arisen in this way.

Despite the attempt to construct an "exact" concept, there may still be a fluctuation or oscillation between the symptoms and the criteria (*PI,* § 79; *Z,* § 439). In fact, in the *Investigations,* Wittgenstein appears to make the point that the situation with scientific concepts is in turn analogous to that with proper names. He says that a name such as "Moses" can be defined by means of various descriptions, but it may be difficult to decide which, if any, of the descriptions is to be definitive, and one will in practice always be ready to revise this decision, should some description prove to be false. But, he adds, the fact that the meaning of the proper name is, so to speak, over-determined, so that one may sometimes use one set of descriptions as definitive and sometimes another set, "detracts as little from its usefulness, as it detracts from that of a table that it stands on four legs instead of three and so sometimes wobbles" (*PI,* § 79; cf. *RFM,* III, § 7). Waismann relates Wittgenstein's views on the role of proof by induction in mathematics (*Introduction to Mathematical Thinking,* p. 96; cf. p. 245). In order to explain the meaning of a proposition which says that something is true of all numbers, one must ask how that proposition is used. What do we regard as a criterion for its truth? "Is the proof by induction," Waismann asks, "only the *symptom* of the fact that the proposition is valid for all numbers? Or do the words 'the proposition is valid for all numbers' mean nothing more than: 'it is true of 1; and if it is true of c, it is also true of $c + 1$?' . . . Actually the proof by induction is the *only* criterion we have."

At this point it will be useful to summarize some characteristics of Wittgenstein's concept of a criterion. Criteria determine the meanings of words (*BB*, p. 57); if one changes the criteria, one changes the meaning (*Z*, § 438). To explain criteria is to give a grammatical explanation, i.e. an explanation of meaning (*BB*, p. 24). Criteria are fixed by convention (*BB*, p. 57; cf. *PI*, §§ 354-355). They determine the language-game with a word, its employment in linguistic discourse, its role in our language (*NL*, p. 286; *PI*, § 182). They are kinds of justification (*BB*, pp. 24-25; cf. pp. 103-104). Finally, criteria are laid down in the rules which determine what counts as adequate justification for the ascription of a concept (*NL*, pp. 286, 293). In his book, *Insight and Illusion*, P.M.S. Hacker has summarized the employment of the term "criterion" in Wittgenstein's later philosophy, and has pointed out the considerable heterogeneity of the kinds of item supposedly connected by the criterial relation. However, he makes two simplifying suggestions (pp. 286-288). First, since the criterial relation is supposed to be a matter of linguistic convention, it is best described as holding between linguistic entities, despite Wittgenstein's variegated usage. Material entities, e.g. phenomena, are thus criteria only in a derivative sense. Second, since the relation concerns the justification for the ascription of a concept, and since both such ascription and such justification will be expressed by means of statements or propositions, the idea of the criteria for a word or concept is also assigned a derivative place: they are "the criteria for the assertion of a sentence in which the relevant word is appropriately employed" (p. 287). Modifying some suggestions made by Gordon Baker (*op. cit.*), the distinction between criteria and symptoms may be summarized as follows:

(i)   *p* is a *criterion* for *q* if *p* is non-inductive evidence for *q*, i.e. if there exists a linguistic convention to the effect that *p* justifies *q*.

(ii)   *p* is a *symptom* for *q* if *p* is inductive evidence for *q*, i.e. if the truth of *p* regularly coincides with the truth of some *p'*, where *p'* is a criterion for *q*.

It can be immediately seen that Wittgenstein's theory of criteria exemplifies the semantic theory described earlier. Criteria are those propositions which are conventionally taken to justify the employment of a sentence, and in this way they establish the meaning of the sentence and so of the words it contains. Such linguistic conventions determining the conditions in which a word may justifiably be ascribed are the rules which constitute the language-game with that word. However, I would like to make the stronger claim that Wittgenstein's discussion of criteria makes precisely the same points as the theses of family resemblance and broad borderlines, and this will be the theme for discussion for the remainder of this chapter. The possibility of a connection between the two discussions has been noticed by W. Gregory Lycan in his recent review of the literature on criteria; he suggests that "a family-resemblance term might well be construed to be one whose applicability is governed by a loose set of criteria, whose members overlap but do not disjunctively constitute a strict definition of the term."[5] While Lycan's suggestion is undoubtedly correct, he cites only one similarity between the theory of criteria and the discussion of family resemblance, namely, that in neither case is the problem to be resolved by attempting to define concepts by means of a disjunctive set of features. A more positive approach follows from the fact that the argument of this essay so far has presented independent evidence that both the discussion of criteria and that of family resemblance involve the idea of grounds for assertions, or, one might say, they are studies in the grammar of justification. Both sources have produced similar results: that what counts as justification for the ascription of a concept is laid down in the linguistic conventions of a language; that grounds need not entail what they justify; that there is no clear distinction between what is a ground and what is not.

The similarity between the two discussions is evident from the discussion of propositions describing physical objects in the *Blue Book* (p. 51), where Wittgenstein says that such propositions admit of a variety of criteria as evidence. However, the domain where the family resemblance thesis and the theory of criteria actually meet is that of human capacities, dispositions, and actions. For instance, in the *Philosophical Investigations* (§164), he considers the concepts of deriving and reading. He says that attempting to find the "essence" of deriving is like stripping the leaves from an artichoke in order to find the "real" plant. On the contrary, what is essential to deriving is not hidden beneath the surface, but the "surface" is one of the family of cases of deriving. He adds: "And in the same way we also use the word 'to read' for a family of cases. And in different circumstances we apply different criteria for a person's reading" (cf. *BB*, p. 125). In the case of capacities, Wittgenstein remarks that "a vast net of family likenesses connects the cases in which the expressions of possibility, 'can', 'to be able to', etc. are used. Certain characteristic features, we may say, appear in these cases in different combinations" (*BB*, p. 117). But, elsewhere, he describes the situation as follows: "The criteria which we accept for 'fitting', 'being able to', 'understanding', are much more complicated than might appear at first sight" (*PI*, §182). This directly supports the conclusion of the previous chapter, that the resemblances which members of a conceptual family bear to one another are "certain characteristic features" whose presence constitutes the justification for the ascription of the concept.

Wittgenstein's discussion of the criteria for saying that someone believes what he says (*BB*, pp. 143-144) was mentioned above. This discussion continues as follows:

> We regard certain facial expressions, gestures, etc. as characteristic for the expression of belief. We speak of a "tone of conviction". And yet it is clear that this tone of conviction isn't always present whenever we rightly speak of conviction. "Just so," you might say, "this shows that there is something else, something behind these gestures, etc. which is the real belief as opposed to mere expressions of belief."—"Not at all," I should say, "many different criteria distinguish, under different circumstances, cases of believing what you say from those of not believing what you say" (p. 144).

Thus, he introduces the notion of a criterion here to make precisely the points made in the discussion of family resemblance; indeed, he subsequently remarks that there is a family of cases of believing what one says (*BB*, p.145). This passage includes several important points: that belief is ascribed on the basis of characteristic behaviour; that a particular criterion need not be present for belief to be correctly ascribed; that there is nothing in common to all cases of belief, and, *a fortiori*, there is no hidden mental state of belief. He also remarks that the evidence on which we ascribe a disposition is corrigible in that it may be contradicted by further evidence (*BB*, pp. 145-146). Elsewhere, Wittgenstein remarks that "the justifications for calling something an expression of doubt, conviction, etc., largely, though of course not wholly, consist in descriptions of gestures, the play of facial expressions, and even the tone of voice" (*BB*, p. 103). Finally, it should be noted that the passage on the employment of proper names and the fluctuation of scientific definitions in the *Philosophical*

Investigations (§ 79) occurs in the middle of Wittgenstein's discussion of family resemblance and broad borderlines. There thus appears to be every reason for identifying the theory of meaning underlying the latter with that underlying the theory of criteria.

The account of Wittgenstein's notion of a "criterion" given in this chapter has placed some degree of emphasis upon the passages in the *Blue Book* which discuss this concept. There are two reasons for this emphasis. The first is that the *Blue Book* offers the clearest exposition of the term in all of his later writings. It has been pointed out that this exposition is not entirely reliable, but it is nevertheless extremely useful when treated with caution and when considered against the background of Wittgenstein's other comments on the matter. The second reason for examining the *Blue Book* concept of a criterion in some detail is that I wished to argue for a unity in this concept throughout Wittgenstein's later philosophy. In particular, I wished to maintain that this concept was entirely consistent with that to be found in the *Philosophical Investigations*, and, indeed, supported the interpretations commonly given of the latter notion. The popular view, that there are two distinct conceptions in the later wirtings, is derived, I allege, from an over-dogmatic interpretation of the central discussion in the *Blue Book* (pp. 24-25), which does not give adequate attention to the context in which this discussion appears. In addition, I wished to consider the thesis of language strata contained in Waismann's writings. This suggests an interpretation of the *Blue Book* concept of a criterion which has a *prima facie* plausibility and some degree of historical support. However, I believe that there are some difficulties in accepting this as an account of the *Blue Book* discussion, and that it is certainly wrong to suppose that a stratified conception of language underlies the concept of a criterion to be found in the *Investigations*.

My main objective in this chapter was to show how the theory of criteria reflected the kind of semantic theory described in the first half of this essay. There is considerable evidence to support this account, and most of Wittgenstein's commentators agree in identifying the criterial relation as one of evidence. My interpretation of the theory of criteria also lent some support to the account given earlier of the term, "language-game". Finally, I wished to argue that the theory of criteria was making precisely the same points as the discussion of family resemblance and broad borderlines, for both concern the "variety of evidences" for our statements. This will, I hope, serve to point out fundamental connections between apparently disparate topics of discourse in Wittgenstein's later philosophy.

Chapter VI

CONCLUSION

It will be useful to conclude this essay by attempting to summarize the course which the arguments have taken, and the various points and problems which have been raised. It was suggested at the beginning of the essay that Wittgenstein's later philosophy started from the fundamental conception that language was to be regarded as an instrument adopted by the convention of a human community to serve its own social ends. This is the conception of language which is to be found in the lecture which Brouwer gave in Vienna in 1928. On this view, words and sentences have the meanings with which a human society chooses to endow them; they derive their sense from the conventions which the community decides to adopt in order to regulate their employment. Consequently, if one wishes to determine the meaning of a word, one has to look and see what rules are laid down on those occurrences where that meaning is explained to someone; these occurrences involve the teaching of the circumstances which are conventionally regarded as appropriate for the employment of the word. Thus, these linguistic conventions, the rules for the use of a word, determine its sense. This aspect of meaning, the fact that language is an activity regulated by conventions, is what is involved when Wittgenstein talks of the *employment* (*Verwendung*) of a word or sentence. He explores this aspect of meaning by exploiting the analogy with a game, and he observes that games, like language, are activities constituted by arbitrarily adopted rules. He wishes to identify a system of such conventions which specify the circumstances of legitimate employment of a word or set of words, which specify what is taken to count as adequate justification for the use of that word or those words, and he calls such a system the "language-game" with those words.

One kind of convention which Wittgenstein singles out for particular study is that which specifies the circumstances under which a predicate may be legitimately ascribed to something, the conditions which are conventionally regarded as justifying the assertion of the sentence which is used to ascribe that predicate. He says that the assertive application of declarative sentences is an essential part of the game which we play with such sentences, in the same way that it is an essential part of a game that the players play with the intention of winning. The grounds which are taken to support such assertions, Wittgenstein calls "criteria". Through our linguistic conventions, the sense of a declarative sentence is specified by the evidences which are regarded as justifying its assertion. Conversely, such conventions endow these criteria with their evidential value.

An important point concerning criteria is that such evidences need not constitute individually necessary and jointly sufficient conditions for the correctness of application of the relevant predicate. They need not be necessary, for there may be a variety of such evidences; there may be a multiplicity of family resemblances connecting the various exemplars of the concept. Such a conception is obviously essential in order to give the correct account of psychological states, for a person may sometimes hide his pains as well as sometimes showing them. Further, it is of the essence of human capacities that we do not demonstrate all of them all of the time, and so some explanation must be offered of how we justifiably ascribe capacities to someone without his demonstrating them at the time of ascription. On the other hand, the evidences for our assertions need not constitute sufficient conditions for their truth: they are corrigible, they may be controverted by subsequent evidence. The grounds for our beliefs need not entail the truth of what we believe, for example. In the case of psychological states, it is also the case that we may mistakenly believe someone to be in pain, because he is simply pretending; we may be justified in ascribing pain to him, but that ascription may subsequently turn out to be false. This corrigibility of our ascriptions may be caused by not being certain what is to count as evidence and what is not: there may be no clear division between essential and in-essential, between sufficient evidence and insufficient evidence, between criteria and symptoms. Consequently, there may be a broad borderline between those cases where a predicate applies, and those where it does not apply; a domain where its applicability is in principle indeterminate without an arbitrary decision with regard to the rules for the predicate employed. However, even though criteria need not constitute decisive evidence for our assertions, they do constitute necessarily good evidence, non-inductive evidence, evidence guaranteed by our linguistic conventions.

These linguistic conventions rest upon our social practices; they are constituted or created by our linguistic acts, which amount to the application (*Anwendung*) of our words and sentences. These have a sense only insofar as they form a part of a technique, insofar as they contribute to a custom or institution. Possessing a concept, understanding a rule, are demonstrated by the person's correct performance, his mastery of a technique. It is to be noted that this position, that the ascription of understanding to a person is to be justified by reference to his behaviour, appears to directly entail the impossibility of a private language, one which refers to a person's private immediate sensations, and which only he can understand. Further, whereas correct performance constitutes criterial evidence for understanding a rule, merely reciting the verbal expression of the rule does not constitute criterial evidence, but is only an empirical correlate of understanding.

Although, at the beginning of this essay, I emphasized

133

that my purpose was to be primarily exegetical, rather than critical, a number of critical observations have been made in the course of the discussion. Now, on Wittgenstein's view, necessity is simply a matter of linguistic convention, and so he is committed to a conventionalist account of meaning. A particularly important conclusion, which was reached in Chapter III, is that, when this conventionalist account of meaning is applied to mathematical propositions, it turns out to be inadequate in principle. For, either it is committed to the doctrine that the sense of a mathematical proposition is determined by its proof, in which case it fails to do justice to the applicability of mathematics; or it is committed to the doctrine that the sense of a mathematical proposition is specified by its application, in which case it fails to account for the role of proof in mathematics. In the years immediately following the Brouwer lecture, Wittgenstein appears to have concentrated upon justification in mathematics, upon the rules defining mathematical systems or calculi, and to have adopted the former position. In his later writings, he emphasizes the application of mathematical propositions, and suggests that they are conventional decisions, akin to "grammatical" propositions. But, if they are conventions, the question arises, *why* should they require proof or justification? And, even more difficult, *how* can they possibly be justified? It is ironic indeed that one of the chief interests and motivations of Wittgenstein's later philosophy should culminate in a result which was apparently hopelessly inadequate.

The conception of language as the product of free human activity also leads to a conception of philosophy which is radically different from the traditional activity which is known by that name. The role of the philosopher is simply to study and describe the linguistic conventions governing the employment of our words and sentences. These conventions are all in plain view; there is nothing new to be found, no discovery to be made, no doctrine to be propounded. All that is necessary is that one pay sufficient attention to language, and not be misled by its surface appearance. Traditional philosophy, on this view, consists in the nonsensical statements people tend to make when they are misled through seeing language in the wrong way. Philosophers believe that they are proposing necessary truths, and in a sense they are correct in this belief; but this is only because their metaphysical propositions hide grammatical rules, and these rules may or may not be those of the actual grammar of our ordinary everyday language. They create problems for themselves through their failure to command a clear view of ordinary language and through imposing their preconceptions upon it. But these are pseudo-problems, to be removed or "dissolved" by making ordinary linguistic usage surveyable.

This suggests a "therapeutic" interpretation of philosophy, as a personal dialectic encounter between therapist and patient. In fact, I have suggested that an underlying theme running through Wittgenstein's later works is that philosophy is only to be justified in terms of this therapeutic purpose. Philosophical methods are to be adopted only insofar as they assist in the removal of misunderstandings. Architectonic projects are ruled out as irrelevant. But, as I indicated in Chapter II, this directs philosophy towards a piecemeal, individual, non-repeatable, unsystematic activity, whereas most philosophers would wish for something global, general, replicable, definitive, and systematic. This difference turns on the problem of the validation of the evidence which a philosopher employs. In the dialectic encounter, the evidence comes from the person who is suffering from philosophical bewilderment. He is made aware of his own employment of the words which cause him difficulty. In the systematic conception, however, the evidence takes the form of normative statements attempting to describe the conventions of a particular society. Such statements must then be validated against the behaviour of the community, in the manner outlined by H.L.A. Hart.[1] But how does this activity differ from lexicography? Why is it not simply a branch of linguistic science? One answer, which is given by P.M.S. Hacker, is that philosophical problems are conceptual, not empirical.[2] Unfortunately, this intuitively plausible distinction is left entirely unexplained. Hacker suggests that the typical form of a conceptual statement or question is modal, but Wittgenstein criticizes this form of expression as confounding grammatical and empirical possibilities and necessities. In fact, he explicitly suggests that, to avoid this confusion, we recast such direct normative statements (i.e. those containing normative operators) in the form of indirect normative statements which describe the employment of particular linguistic items in a particular language-game.[3] And such statements are precisely the kind of evidence which would be employed in an empirical investigation of a language. So an additional argument for the therapeutic, dialectic conception of philosophy would be that the alternative is no longer philosophy, but linguistics.

Finally, how far does Wittgenstein satisfy his own requirements? Does he impose a preconceived idea onto language, does he make assertions or propose theses? Superficially, he appears to make a great many substantial claims concerning the nature of language. But many of these are not directly in conflict with his conception of philosophy, as they arise in the course of the treatment of particular cases of bewilderment. For example, in criticizing the idea that there must be something in common which justifies the employment of formal concepts, or in the ascription of capacities, he produces several interesting conclusions, which were considered in Chapter IV. And in his criticisms of the possibility of a private language, he appears to make several important claims; the impossibility of such a language would itself be of profound importance. However, all these cases are intended as examples of the applicability of his method to particular problems. Wittgenstein says that his activity gets its purpose solely from such philosophical problems. Further, some of the assertions which have been drawn from the last two chapters are only of a negative character. For instance, the evidence for one's assertions *need not* take the form of necessary and sufficient conditions for their truth. At one level this attacks a philosophical requirement, but at another it rejects a philosophical theory of meaning. So, what of his own conception of meaning and language? This appears to rest upon his "look and see" strategy, and in this case appears to be quite harmless. For it simply is the case that one says of someone that he knows the meaning of a particular word or sentence if he demonstrates the ability to employ it under the circumstances which are generally taken as appropriate; if he regards himself as justified in so doing; if he can cite those circumstances as justification for his utterances; if he criticizes other people's use of those utterances by reference to those conditions; if he explains the use of the word or sentence to others by attempting to characterize such conditions; and so on. These characteristics may simply be the bed-rock of our conventions: to describe them may be merely to give some remarks on the use of the word "meaning". But such remarks also appear to be a solid foundation on which to develop a conception of philosophy and a philosophy of language.

NOTES

Chapter I

1. See B.F. McGuinness' preface to *Ludwig Wittgenstein und der Wiener Kreis (WWK)*, p. 16. Full details of all references are given in the Bibliography.
2. L.E.J. Brouwer, "Mathematik, Wissenschaft und Sprache."
3. See McGuinness' preface to *WWK*, p. 13.
4. See, especially, S.E. Toulmin, "Ludwig Wittgenstein."
5. M. Dummett, "The Reality of the Past"; "Truth"; "Wittgenstein's Philosophy of Mathematics."
6. G.P. Baker, *The Logic of Vagueness.*

Chapter II

1. K.T. Fann, *Wittgenstein's Conception of Philosophy*, especially chaps. VI and IX.
2. P.M.S. Hacker, *Insight and Illusion: Wittgenstein on Philosophy and the Metaphysics of Experience*, chap. V.
3. L.E.J. Brouwer, "Mathematik, Wissenschaft und Sprache." Summarized in Hacker, op. cit., pp. 100-102; and in G.T. Kneebone, *Mathematical Logic and the Foundations of Mathematics*, pp. 319-321.
4. L.E.J. Brouwer, "Consciousness, Philosophy, and Mathematics."
5. A. Heyting, "Die intuitionistische Grundlegung der Mathematik." English translation in P. Benacerraf and H. Putnam (Eds.), *Philosophy of Mathematics: Selected Readings.*
6. See McGuinness' preface to *WWK*, p. 16.
7. H. Feigl, as quoted in G. Pitcher, *The Philosophy of Wittgenstein*, p. 8 n.; cf. von Wright, "Biographical Sketch."
8. Brouwer, "Consciousness, Philosophy, and Mathematics."
9. For a further discussion of the concepts of alienable and inalienable possession, see A.J.P. Kenny, "The Verification Principle and the Private Language Argument."
10. E.g. J. Wisdom, "Other Minds (I)."
11. B.A. Farrell, "An Appraisal of Therapeutic Positivism. (I)." For Wittgenstein's reaction, see K. Britton, "Portrait of a Philosopher"; N. Malcolm, *Ludwig Wittgenstein: A Memoir*, pp. 56-57.

12. CF. G. Frege, "The Thought: A Logical Inquiry."
13. That the assertive use of language is but one use among many is obscured by several accounts of the constructivist position. For instance, C.F. Kielkopf says that on this view the philosopher simply has to be clear about what goes on when people make assertions (*Strict Finitism*, p. 24). There are at least two reasons why this has not been made explicit. First, most of the writers who have concerned themselves with the realist/constructivist opposition have been interested in the philosophy of mathematics, and have characterized mathematical theorems as assertions to be justified by proofs (e.g. Dummett, Kielkopf). This does not accord very well with Wittgenstein's philosophy of mathematics, which characterizes theorems as grammatical rules, and, in general, assimilating all uses of language to assertion is as "explanatory" as assimilating all uses to fact-stating. Second, some writers have defined the problem in terms of the meaning of statements, and have thus evaded the difficulty of giving an account of other types of sentence. But if constructivism is to be set up as a *general* theory of meaning, there is no reason for identifying assertion as a primary object of interest.
14. Some philosophers who offer a critique of mathematics do not see themselves as destroying anything of any importance. Thus, Heyting suggests that he is carrying out "the excision of noxious ornaments, beautiful in form, but hollow in substance" (*Intuitionism: An Introduction*, pp. 10-11).

Chapter III

1. Cf. W.G. Lycan's "Noninductive Evidence: Recent Work on Wittgenstein's 'Criteria'," which points out that a paradigm case for teaching someone else the meaning of a word is at the same time a paradigm case for demonstrating one's own knowledge of that meaning.
2. See A. Sloman, "Exploring Logical Necessity." Sloman identifies this as the basic idea behind extreme versions of conventionalism.
3. See M. Dummett, "Truth," for an elaboration of these themes.
4. See also Heyting, *Intuitionism: An Introduction*, p. 101 f.
5. This remark is assessed by Charles F. Kielkopf in his book, *Strict Finitism* (chap. 5).
6. In *Translations from the Philosophical Writings of Gottlob Frege*, ed. P.T. Geach and M. Black, pp. 182-233.
7. This example is contained in Waismann's *Introduction to Mathematical Thinking* (p. 98), but was taken from a manuscript

THE GRAMMAR OF JUSTIFICATION

which Wittgenstein permitted Waismann to use. The philosophy of mathematics contained in this book is clearly influenced by Wittgenstein's own ideas to a considerable extent. See, especially, chap. 9, "Present Status of the Investigation of the Foundations"; chap. 16, "Inventing or Discovering?"; and "Epilogue," p. 245.

8. See also Waismann, op. cit., p. 119.
9. This passage from Waismann's book appears to have been based upon remarks which Wittgenstein included in the *Philosophische Bemerkungen* (§114).
10. See A.J.P. Kenny, "The Verification Principle and the Private Language Argument," p. 211, and n. 11, p. 281, referring to *BB*, pp. 12, 96-97.

Chapter IV

1. M.A. Simon, "When is a Resemblance a Family Resemblance?"
2. H. Wennerberg, "The Concept of Family Resemblance in Wittgenstein's Later Philosophy."
3. See the papers by Pompa, Simon, and Wennerberg, and also A. Manser, "Games and Family Resemblances."
4. R. Bambrough, "Universals and Family Resemblances."
5. W.E. Kennick, "Philosophy as Grammar and the Reality of Universals"; R.J. Richman, "Something Common."
6. The interpretation of Aristotle's doctrine given here is derived largely from the study by J. Owens, *The Doctrine of Being in the Aristotelian* Metaphysics, chap. 3, which offers the clearest account of the doctrine of equivocals available. Standard abbreviations are used for referring to Aristotle's works. Wittgenstein himself claimed never to have read a single word of Aristotle; see K. Britton, "Portrait of a Philosopher."
7. The contributor to J.M. Baldwin's *Dictionary of Philosophy and Psychology* (p. 739) even alleges that Aristotle talked of concepts forming a family, but this seems to be merely a too strict translation of *"aph enos"* ("having a common origin").
8. G. Frege, *Grundgesetze der Arithmetik*, Vol. II, §56. In *Translations from the Philosophical Writings of Gottlob Frege*, ed. P.T. Geach and M. Black, p. 159.
9. H. Khatchadourian, "Vagueness"; "Vagueness, Meaning, and Absurdity"; "Vagueness, Verifiability, and Metaphysics."
10. Cf. P.M.S. Hacker, *Insight and Illusion*, p. 184.
11. E.g. W.P. Alston, "Vagueness."
12. Cf. G. Frege, "On the Foundations of Geometry."

13. M. Dummett, "The Philosophical Significance of Gödel's Theorem." Cf. Heyting, *Intuitionism: An Introduction,* pp. 106, 116.

14. A comparison of pages 3 and 4 of the *Blue Book* suggests that Frege might have been a possible target here. This is supported by the fact that Waismann cites as one of four
th theses constituting Frege's philosophy of mathematics the position that the sense of an arithmetic symbol is to be explicated in terms of the mental process of thinking (*Introduction to Mathematical Thinking,* p. 238). Further, Waismann gives an argument of Wittgenstein's to attack this thesis. However, this philosophical position is quite inconsistent with Frege's general anti-psychologistic attitude. See, for example, *Foundations of Arithmetic,* p. x; §26. Nevertheless, Frege's approach does share with this position the view that something other than the use of signs is necessary to give an account of their sense.

Chapter V

1. P.M.S. Hacker, *Insight and Illusion,* pp. 288-289.

2. F. Waismann, "Language Strata"; "The Many-Level Structure of Language"; "Verifiability." Cf. *WWK,* pp. 19-22.

3. Hacker, op. cit., pp. 306-308; see also *PI,* §§377-388.

4. In a discussion of the concept of numerical equivalence taken from one of Wittgenstein's manuscripts, Waismann considers the "various criteria used for the expression 'numerically equivalent'." See his *Introduction to Mathematical Thinking,* p. 111, and cf. p. 245.

5. W.G. Lycan, "Noninductive Evidence: Recent Work on Wittgenstein's 'Criteria'."

Chapter VI

1. H.L.A. Hart, *The Concept of Law,* pp. 9-11, 50-54.

2. P.M.S. Hacker, *Insight and Illusion,* p. 121. Cf. *Z,* §458.

3. , *Z,* §134. For the distinction between "direct" and "indirect" normative statements, see J. Raz, *The Concept of a Legal System,* p. 49.

BIBLIOGRAPHY

I. Works by Wittgenstein (in order of composition).

Notebooks 1914-1916. Ed. G.H. von Wright and G.E.M. Anscombe. Trans. G.E.M. Anscombe (Oxford: Blackwell) 1961.

Tractatus Logico-Philosophicus. Trans. D.F. Pears and B.F. McGuinness (London: Routledge and Kegan Paul) 1961.

Ludwig Wittgenstein und der Wiener Kreis. Shorthand notes recorded by F. Waismann. Ed. B.F. McGuinness (Oxford: Blackwell) 1967.

Philosophische Bemerkungen. Ed. R. Rhees (Oxford: Blackwell) 1964.

"Wittgenstein's Lectures in 1930-33," by G.E. Moore. Part I: *Mind,* 63 (1954), 1-15; Part II: ibid., 63 (1954), 289-316; Part III: ibid., 64 (1955), 1-27.

Philosophische Grammatik. Ed. R. Rhees (Oxford: Blackwell) 1969.

The Blue and Brown Books (Oxford: Blackwell) 1958.

"Notes for Lectures on 'Private Experience' and 'Sense Data'." Ed. and trans. R. Rhees. *Philosophical Review,* 77 (1968), 275-320.

Remarks on the Foundations of Mathematics. Ed. G.H. von Wright, R. Rhees, and G.E.M. Anscombe. Trans. G.E.M. Anscombe. 2nd edn. (Oxford: Blackwell) 1967.

Philosophical Investigations. Ed. G.E.M. Anscombe and R. Rhees. Trans. G.E.M. Anscombe. 3rd edn. (Oxford: Blackwell) 1967.

Zettel. Ed. G.E.M. Anscombe and G.H. von Wright. Trans. G.E.M. Anscombe (Oxford: Blackwell) 1967.

On Certainty. Ed. G.E.M. Anscombe and G.H. von Wright. Trans. D. Paul and G.E.M. Anscombe (Oxford: Blackwell) 1969.

II. Other items cited in the text.

Albritton, R. "On Wittgenstein's Use of the Term 'Criterion'." *Journal of Philosophy,* 56 (1959), 845-857.

Alston, W.P. "Vagueness." In The *Encyclopedia of Philosophy,* ed. P. Edwards (New York: Macmillan) 1967.

Aristotle. *The Works of Aristotle.* Ed. and trans. W.D. Ross (London: Oxford University Press).

Baker, G.P. *The Logic of Vagueness.* Unpublished D. Phil. thesis (Oxford University) 1970.

BIBLIOGRAPHY

Baldwin, J.M., ed. *Dictionary of Philosophy and Psychology.* (New York: Macmillan) 1901.

Bambrough, R. "Universals and Family Resemblance." *Proceedings of the Aristotelian Society*, 61 (1960-1961), 207-222.

Benacerraf, P., and Putnam, H., eds. *Philosophy of Mathematics: Selected Readings* (Englewood Cliffs, N.J.: Prentice-Hall) 1964.

Black, M. "Vagueness: An Exercise in Logical Analysis." *Philosophy of Science*, 4 (1937), 427-455.

Britton, K. "Portrait of a Philosopher." *The Listener*, 10 June 1955, 1071-1072.

Brouwer, L.E.J. "Consciousness, Philosophy, and Mathematics." *Proceedings of the Tenth International Congress of Philosophy*, Amsterdam, 1940, 1235-1249.

Brouwer, L.E.J. "Mathematik, Wissenschaft und Sprache." *Monatshefte für Mathematik und Physik*, 36 (1929), 153-164.

Clegg, J.S. "Symptoms." *Analysis*, 32 (1972), 90-98.

Dummett, M. "The Philosophical Significance of Gödel's Theorem." *Ratio*, 5 (1963), 140-155.

Dummett, M. "The Reality of the Past." *Proceedings of the Aristotelian Society*, 69 (1968-1969), 239-258.

Dummett, M. "Truth." *Proceedings of the Aristotelian Society*, 59 (1958-1959), 141-162.

Dummett, M. "Wittgenstein's Philosophy of Mathematics." *Philosophical Review*, 68 (1959), 324-348.

Fann, K.T. *Wittgenstein's Conception of Philosophy* (Oxford: Blackwell) 1969.

Farrell, B.A. "An Appraisal of Therapeutic Positivism. (I)." *Mind*, 55 (1946), 25-48.

Frege, G. *The Foundations of Arithmetic.* Trans. J.L. Austin (Oxford: Blackwell) 1950.

Frege, G. *Grundgesetze der Arithmetik* (Olms: Hildesheim) 1962.

Frege, G. "On the Foundations of Geometry." Trans. M.E. Szabo. *Philosophical Review*, 69 (1960), 3-17.

Frege, G. "The Thought: A Logical Inquiry." Trans. A.M. and M. Quinton. *Mind*, 65 (1956), 289-311.

Frege, G. *Translations from the Philosophical Writings of Gottlob Frege.* Ed. P.T. Geach and M. Black. 2nd edn. (Oxford: Blackwell) 1960.

Hacker, P.M.S. *Insight and Illusion: Wittgenstein on Philosophy and the Metaphysics of Experience* (London: Oxford University Press) 1972.

Hart, H.L.A. *The Concept of Law* (London: Oxford University Press) 1961.

Heyting, A. "Die intuitionistische Grundlegung der Mathematik." *Erkenntnis*, 2 (1931), 106-115.

Heyting, A. *Intuitionism: An Introduction.* 3rd edn. (Amsterdam: North-Holland) 1971.

Hospers, J. *Introduction to Philosophical Analysis* (Englewood Cliffs, N.J.: Prentice-Hall) 1953.

Katz, J.J. *The Philosophy of Language* (New York: Harper and Row) 1966.

Kennick, W.E. "Philosophy as Grammar and the Reality of Universals." In *Ludwig Wittgenstein: Philosophy and Language*, ed. A. Ambrose and M. Lazerowitz (London: Allen and Unwin) 1972. Pp. 140-185.

Kenny, A.J.P. "Criterion." In *The Encyclopedia of Philosophy*, ed. P. Edwards (New York: Macmillan) 1967.

Kenny, A.J.P. "The Verification Principle and the Private Language Argument." In *The Private Language Argument*, ed. O.R. Jones (London: Macmillan) 1971. Pp. 204-228.

Khatchadourian, H. "Vagueness." *Philosophical Quarterly*, 12 (1962), 138-152.

Khatchadourian, H. "Vagueness, Meaning, and Absurdity." *American Philosophical Quarterly*, 2 (1965), 119-129.

Khatchadourian, H. "Vagueness, Verifiability, and Metaphysics." *Foundations of Language*, 1 (1965), 249-267.

Kielkopf, C.F. *Strict Finitism* (The Hague: Mouton) 1970.

Kneebone, G.T. *Mathematical Logic and the Foundations of Mathematics* (Princeton, N.J.: Van Nostrand) 1963.

Lycan, W.G. "Noninductive Evidence: Recent Work on Wittgenstein's 'Criteria'." *American Philosophical Quarterly*, 8 (1971), 109-125.

Malcolm, N. *Ludwig Wittgenstein: A Memoir* (London: Oxford University Press) 1958.

Manser, A. "Games and Family Resemblances." *Philosophy*, 42 (1967), 210-225.

Owens, J. *The Doctrine of Being in the Aristotelian Metaphysics.* 2nd edn. (Toronto: Pontifical Institute of Mediaeval Studies) 1963.

Pitcher, G. *The Philosophy of Wittgenstein* (Englewood Cliffs, N.J.: Prentice-Hall) 1964.

Pollock, J.L. "Criteria and Our Knowledge of the Material World." *Philosophical Review*, 76 (1967), 28-60.

Pompa, L. "Family Resemblance." *Philosophical Quarterly*, 17 (1967), 63-69.

Raz, J. *The Concept of a Legal System* (London: Oxford University Press) 1970.

Richman, R.J. "Something Common." *Journal of Philosophy,* 59 (1962), 821-830.

Rundle, B. *Perception, Sensation, and Verification* (London: Oxford University Press) 1972.

Simon, M.A. "When is a Resemblance a Family Resemblance?" *Mind,* 78 (1969), 408-416.

Sloman, A. "Explaining Logical Necessity." *Proceedings of the Aristotelian Society,* 69 (1968-1969), 33-50.

Toulmin, S.E. "Ludwig Wittgenstein." *Encounter,* January 1969, pp. 58-71.

Waismann, F. *Introduction to Mathematical Thinking* (New York: Ungar, and London: Hafner) 1951.

Waismann, F. "Language Strata." In *Logic and Language,* ed. A.G.N. Flew. 2nd Ser. (Oxford: Blackwell) 1953. Chap. 1, pp. 11-31.

Waismann, F. "The Many-Level Structure of Language." *Synthese,* 5 (1946), 211-219 (sometimes 221-229).

Waismann, F. *The Principles of Linguistic Philosophy.* Ed. R. Harre (London: Macmillan) 1965.

Waismann, F. "Verifiability." *Proceedings of the Aristotelian Society,* Supp. Vol. 19 (1945), 119-150.

Wennerberg, H. "The Concept of Family Resemblance in Wittgenstein's Later Philosophy." *Theoria,* 33 (1967), 107-132.

Wisdom, J. "Other Minds (I)." *Mind,* 49 (1940), 369-402.

von Wright, G.H. "Biographical Sketch." In *Ludwig Wittgenstein: A Memoir,* by N. Malcolm, pp. 1-22.

INDEX